I0011243

Requirements Development Guidebook

V 1.1

Dahlia Biazid

Copyright © 2015 Dahlia Biazid, Reqmaster

All Rights Reserved.

No part of this book may be reproduced, or stored in a retrieval system, or transmitted in any form or by any means, electronic, mechanical, photocopying, recording, or otherwise, without express written permission of the publisher.

TABLE OF CONTENTS

SECTION I

INTRODUCTION

About this Book

If you are a Business Analyst, the following questions will certainly mean something to you. You've probably asked yourself these questions at one point or another when you were assigned your early requirements development tasks.

How do I know I covered all the requirements? Where do I begin? When should I stop? Did I miss something that will result in unpleasant surprises down the road?

You might have been taught (*or not*) good elicitation techniques, such as how to efficiently run an interview, facilitate a workshop, or prepare a questionnaire. You might have also been introduced to valuable analysis and communication techniques, such as how to write a use case, draw a class diagram, arrange business rules in a decision tree, and so forth.

So far so good! But do you know how to proceed from there? Do you know how to put the pieces together beginning-to-end in a meaningful journey?

Most analysts that I have met rely on trial and error until they develop an intuition about what comes first and what goes next. They struggle on their own to piece together the information.

They mostly follow the lead of the information dumped on them from the client, and work on parts here and parts there until the requirements "seem" complete, hoping to magically cover all that needs to be covered.

The practice of Requirements Development (which is the focus in this book) employs plenty of tools and techniques that remain scattered in toolboxes, often without a coherent structure. Some organize requirements (and techniques) in views, aspects, or models, such as the UI aspect, the function aspect, the data aspect, the process aspect, and so on. This is obviously a step forward, but it still does not fully solve the problem, you need a complete map to guide the requirements development work from beginning to end. The absence of a recognized structured method to follow in requirements development work remains a challenge for most analysts today.

Automation requirements development work should be guided by a systematic strategy or plan that has a concrete beginning, a clear direction, and a logical order to construct a complete requirements deliverable in the most efficient way.

This book suggests a model for analysts to use when developing requirements for automation projects. Think of it as a cookbook with recipes. In this book, I will outline a beginning-to-end roadmap to guide you through the requirements development journey in order to ensure that your analysis is evolving in the right direction towards requirements maturity and completion. This will help you avoid overlooking or misunderstanding requirements.

The roadmap presented in this book does not introduce new techniques; rather, it arranges the existing ones in a logical and meaningful order. The roadmap puts the pieces together to form a plan that can serve you at different levels of your professional experience. It can also be used as an elicitation plan. I will show you the model in the form of a comprehensive yet brief tutorial. You may use the titles of the station in the roadmap as guidance, or use the content in each station to analyze each aspect of the requirements.

Who Should Read this Book?

The roadmap in this book draws on the foundational knowledge of Business Analysis.

If you are a new analyst, you are expected to have a basic understanding of the different requirements development techniques, such as elicitation techniques (e.g. interviews and observation), or analysis and communication techniques (e.g. class diagrams and use cases).

This roadmap is a framework that organizes the techniques that the reader already knows; it will not explain the techniques themselves. Since many books have already elaborated on the various techniques, instead of repeating the same information, I will briefly describe the technique usage and its relevant special considerations in the Tools Section. References to other resources that contain in-depth information about the different techniques will be also suggested in that chapter.

If you are an experienced analyst, you may choose to use this roadmap as an easy formula in your work.

Requirements Development: Exactly What Is It?

1. Inside Requirements Development

Requirements development is a broad concept that describes various activities performed in order to deliver a set (or sets) of requirements. These are the three components of requirements development:

1. Discovery (also known as elicitation), with its various available techniques such as interviews, workshops, documentation analysis, and observation.
2. Analysis, which includes the effort to complete, organize and

classify the collected information, analysis of the interrelationships and the reciprocated impacts among requirements, uncovering conflicts and unspoken needs, reconciling needs, and so on.

3. Documentation of the analyzed requirements in a body of coherent deliverable crafted in a way that makes sense to different groups of stakeholders – such as business users and managers, and solution teams – in a concise, effective, and clear way.

> Note 1: Unfortunately, many analysts underestimate the value of the analysis and skip over this step straight to documentation. I cannot emphasize enough how important and useful the analysis step is. Obviously, documentation itself is an analysis tool but it is not enough. If you want to find insights and hidden treasures (or pitfalls), you must at some point, sit by yourself with the material you have and see if you can toy around with it to come up with new insights. Analysis is a fundamental component of requirements development and the essence of the analyst job. Don't underestimate its value.

The official Capability Maturity Model Integration (CMMI) website[1] describes the different phases of the requirements development work as follows:

"Requirements are the basis for design. The development of requirements includes the following activities:

- *Elicitation, analysis, validation, and communication of customer needs, expectations, and constraints to obtain customer requirements that constitute an understanding of what will satisfy stakeholders*
- *Collection and coordination of stakeholder needs*
- *Development of the lifecycle requirements of the product*
- *Establishment of the customer requirements*
- *Establishment of initial product and product component re-*

---

quirements consistent with customer requirements
This process area addresses all customer requirements rather
than only product-level requirements because the customer may
also provide specific design requirements."

2. Requirements Development in Context

Requirements Development and Requirements Management are
the two pillars of Requirements Engineering. Requirements Engineering itself is part of the larger discipline of Business Analysis,
which as the name suggests, extends beyond requirements work.
It can include Process Improvement and Management, Enterprise
Architecture, and Analytics. Requirements Engineering is also
part of the Software Engineering discipline, which covers other
areas such as Software Development and Testing. So in a way,
Requirements Engineering sits between Business Analysis and
Software Engineering.

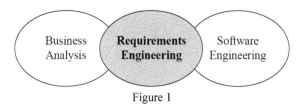

Figure 1

Requirements Development is also one of a number of equally
important and interrelated activity areas. The following illustration shows the requirements development placed among the other
activity areas:

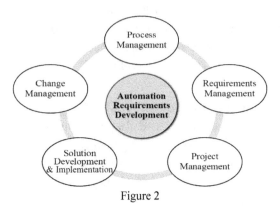

Figure 2

This book focuses on the aspects specifically related to Requirements Development, aside from any management aspects, be they Project Management, Process Management, Requirements Management, or Change Management. This does not imply an undervaluation of those activities, but rather an attempt to give enough attention to the effort of requirements construction without mixing it with the other parallel activities.

Why Do We Need this?

Six Reasons Why a Requirements Development Framework Is Needed

Automation projects vary in their purpose and scope, the nature of the business they address, the time allocated to them, the used technology, and the project type (e.g., developed from scratch products, customized off-shelf products, or revamped systems). Projects may also vary in terms of the applied Business Analysis involvement approach; whether the Business Analyst (BA) is involved from the beginning of the project at the problem definition and solution selection phase or at a later time to help users define their needs (particularly the automation-specific needs). Regardless of the project nature, characteristics, or timing of the BA participation, analysts need a framework to work within and to use to organize their activities (and tailor it, if needed).

1. No Requirements Development Methodology

Requirements development is a critical component of the Software Development Lifecycle and the heart of the Requirements Engineering field. There are no published methodologies specific to Requirements Development. The topic is usually addressed as a part of the software development or the requirements engineering methodologies. Most available literature on the subject of Requirements Engineering combines the Requirements Development techniques with the requirements management concepts. For example, a book may have a chapter about running interviews (an elicitation technique that constitutes a part of Requirements Development), another chapter about use cases (an analysis and communication technique that is also part of Requirements Development), and another chapter about traceability (part of Requirements Management).

This is both reasonable and useful; analysts must be aware of both dimensions of the requirements engineering work at all times. However, it confuses the analyst and leaves the area of requirements development without the focus it deserves.

2. Toolbox and No Strategy

When analysts learn Business Analysis, they are introduced to different valuable techniques, including modeling techniques such as activity diagrams and class diagrams, analysis and documentation techniques (e.g., use cases and data dictionaries), and elicitation techniques (e.g., interviews and observation). They are also introduced to Requirements Management concepts (e.g., scope and change management).

These techniques and concepts are essential and extremely valuable. However, they are, unfortunately, not enough to perform the task at hand. These techniques and concepts are typically taught as separate parts scattered in a toolbox without a strategy that guides analysts.

This approach does not address key questions that can have tremendous impact on the progress of the analysis work. For example, questions like, "When is the best time in the project to use a particular technique?" or "How do I efficiently organize the analysis effort to ensure that no component is overlooked – or discovered when it is too late in the process?" are not addressed. It is the analyst's responsibility to assemble the bits and pieces, to mix and match the techniques, and make decisions about when and where to fit them in order to (eventually and seemingly magically) construct a complete picture.

A roadmap will offer a defined route that organizes and links the techniques and guides the Requirements Development work step by step to ensure efficiency and completion.

3. Inconsistent Success Rates

Because the strategy is still left to the analysts to develop without much guidance, the overall success of the project relies heavily on the analyst's experience and skills. There needs to be a recipe that helps organizations achieve an acceptable level of success and quality independent of the analyst assigned and thus guarantee a more consistent projects success rate.

4. Reliance on Templates, a Second Best Choice

Due to the absence of a methodology specific to requirements development, many organizations must rely on templates to guarantee a reasonable standard of requirements coverage. Although this compromise has helped, and good templates can indeed provide a good reference for requirements work, they still focus on how to deliver the collected information, not on how to find and complete the information as quickly, completely, accurately, and effectively as possible. Moreover, there is no guarantee that the templates are in fact filled with the correct requirements. Templates cannot replace a roadmap that guides the thinking process throughout the requirements process, a navigation map that safeguards against overlooking or misunderstanding requirements.

5. Requirements from an Art to a Science

Requirements development, as a part of the Requirements "Engineering" science, cannot remain subject to the individual skills. Requirements work should follow structured methodologies and defined methods in order to really become a science (if only partially). As long as success is dependent on the analyst's skills and their ability to conceptualize a strategy, it will remain an art. While an art component will and should remain integral to analysis work, in order to move the discipline to its next level of maturity, recognized methods must be defined.

Methods, like the one suggested in this book, will enable and facilitate this transition, so that Business Analysts spend less effort on the technicalities of the requirements work and focus on the real value of Business Analysis: Reform.

6. Guide Users

The role of the analyst is to help users define their needs, and one of the best ways to achieve this is to stimulate users' imagination and thinking process by asking questions to complete the information and find out what lies beyond what is being asked. Users (or solution designers, for that matter) may not recall information or think about issues and needs until the questions are posed to them and they are forced to attentively consider them and come up with clear answers. The clearer the questions, the clearer the answers, and the more organized they are, the more efficient the process.

About the Roadmap

1. What It Is

The Automation Requirements Development Roadmap is a plan carefully prepared to guide the requirements development work from start to finish. You may also consider it to be a complete elicitation plan – even though the roadmap addresses the three components of requirements development (elicitation, analysis, and documentation).

2. The Roadmap Structure

The roadmap is a series of stations logically ordered to ensure the right information is captured at the right time. Each station is concerned with completing a distinct objective and suggests specific activities that lead to that objective.

The stations are grouped into three main phases, with the core phase divided into two sub-phases, as shown in the figure:

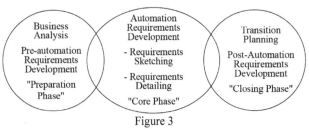

Figure 3

- The Business Analysis phase is a preparatory phase during which you are advised to refrain from thinking about the automation requirements and rather focus on understanding the context of the project from a pure business perspective. Get a feel of the source business problem and context, the background, and the environment in which the solution will operate.
- The Automation Requirements Development phase is the core of your work, where you develop the end solution requirements. To construct the requirements in a logically evolving way and allow for better scope definition at the early stage of the project, the phase is divided into two sub-phases: the requirements sketching phase and the detailing phase.
- The Transition Planning phase is a closing phase, where you prepare for the smooth transition from the old to the new operating model.

3. Inside the Stations

At each station of the roadmap, I will first indicate the target objective and why you need to think about that particular objective at that specific point in time. Then I will show you how to complete that objective using various techniques. These techniques will be categorized under the three requirements development components:

- Elicitation: Which elicitation techniques will best serve the objective of the station and which questions to ask in order to capture the information you need.
- Analysis: Which analysis tools to apply in order to analyze the information from different angles. Whenever possible, I will suggest multiple techniques to allow you to make your own choice depending on your preference.
- Documentation: I then conclude by suggesting how to best document the output of the exercise that you just performed. I will not, however, show complete requirements examples. How to communicate requirements is a topic that warrants its own book, and therefore is not part of this one. Because often the documentation techniques are in themselves analysis instruments (for example, you can use diagrams and use cases to both analyze and document requirements), the same technique may be listed under both analysis and documentation.

4. Questions and Answers about the Roadmap

How does the roadmap intersect with the project phases?
The roadmap is a foundation for the requirements development activity as a distinct practice in one continuum from beginning to end. It follows a parallel but separate "Business Analysis" cycle relatively independent from the project cycle. The roadmap may or may not match up exactly to the project lifecycle phases. It may also overlap or cut across multiple ones.

Is the roadmap more suitable for certain Software Development Lifecycles (SDLC) and not other?
The roadmap suggests a way of thinking and a guide to the analysis approach. It does not matter if the adopted SDLC is plan-driven

(e.g., Waterfall) or change-driven (e.g., Agile). You still perform the same activities either way, only in longer or shorter cycles. The output that you produce may also be consolidated in one complete deliverable (plan-driven) or divided into small separate deliverables (change-driven). That being said, the roadmap assumes that some documentation is produced. In projects that apply extreme agile methods where no documentation is produced, such as XP, you may skip the documentation part of the roadmap, but the logic of the remaining components (particularly the objectives) still applies. If you rely on collaborative sessions to elicit requirements, make sure you cover the areas suggested in the roadmap at some point, either during the sessions or after.

Is every station a clear-cut one?
Yes and no.

Similar to all requirements-related work, the roadmap phases and the order of stations are more suggestive guidelines than hard-and-fast rules. You might find yourself returning to a previous station to review a starting point or think ahead about elements that will be covered in a following phase. This is both normal and acceptable. Do, however, make sure that you complete the objective at hand before you move to the next one. Park the other information for further analysis when you reach that station. Try not to combine focus on many elements at the same time so that every component gets its fair share of analysis and exploration.

How strict do I need to be in applying the roadmap?
Keep your focus but be flexible.

Understandably, users do not typically state clear-cut requirements, but rather tell stories loaded with different pieces of information. Their stories are an assortment of processes and procedures, business rules, data, background information, etc. It is the analyst's responsibility to unbundle this information and place every piece in its appropriate bucket.

At the early stages of the project, give your stakeholders the space to tell their stories as they wish, so you can get a sense of the whole picture. Avoid limiting the discussion prematurely. You want to get a sense of the overall picture and understand the situation from the user's perspective so you can represent them throughout the process.

As you move further in the process, begin to direct the users by identifying the objectives on which you are working. They may still divert from these objectives at some points and include irrelevant information. This is fine as long as the diversion does not hijack the objective at hand. Extract the relevant parts to complete the objective and park the irrelevant ones for examination later. For example, as a user describes the way they perform a task, it is likely that they mention some business rules that guide their processing. As they do so, take notes of those business rules, but stay focused on the task logic and steps. Use your notes when you reach the business rules station and do further probing and analysis, see if you can validate and complete any gaps that may have been missed to ensure that you cover all the variations and cases.

This approach is not only useful to guide your analysis but also to allow for "information recycling." Coming back to information is a great way to ensure the completion and validation of the information. When the same topic is visited more than once, users will be able to think of more details, correct wrong assumptions, and give their requirements better concrete shapes.

There are times when you will find that you can switch a station with another one. I will be highlighting the areas where I think the order may be changed and a station may be interchanged with another one. If you switch stations, keep these two points in mind: First, do not interchange stations outside the same phase; stay within the same phase as much as possible to maintain the same level of detailing. Second, review the stations at the end of each phase to make sure you covered them all and didn't miss any.

Note 2: Sometimes, decisions about certain points are postponed until further information is acquired or other people are involved. If you find yourself dealing with a point that cannot be closed immediately - unless the following exercises depend on it - park it under pending issues for further investigation, and move to the next station.

Is using the roadmap a time overhead?

Following the roadmap shouldn't need more time. The roadmap only organizes and structures the requirements development process. It doesn't add more tasks. To the opposite, organizing your analysis approach as suggested is likely to save you time. The roadmap is carefully organized so that you can capture requirements that affect the scope before you dive into the details, which allows you to move from one requirements maturity level to the next in a logical way. By doing so, you will also be saving on the time often wasted in patching a gap in requirements later in the project. You will be sparing yourself and the team not only the overhead of wasted time, but also the financial cost, team frustration, and any harm that may affect customer relations.

Can I apply the roadmap under the pressure of tight deadlines?

What if tight deadlines get in the way of completing all the stations in the roadmap? I suggest you try to cover all the relevant objectives, if only briefly. If for one reason or another, you can't and you find yourself having to skip stations to wrap up the requirements work, make sure you point out the areas that you have not visited to the consumers of your requirements deliverable. Do not leave the uncovered areas as empty slots for different people to fill with assumptions. Highlight them as open issues. Your job is to ask questions and look for answers. If you are unable to find the answers, do at least the first half of your job and ask the questions.

Will I use all the exercises every time?

The roadmap covers the full range of an automation project. I do not, however, expect that you will use all the stations in all projects. Some stations may be relevant in one project, while in other projects you may find yourself using different parts.

The idea is to give thought to everything but not necessarily apply them all. You shouldn't rely only on what the users present to you. It is possible that they overlook something, and you carry the responsibility to uncover those areas by asking questions. I highly recommend that you stop and give every objective careful thought before you make a judgment about the objective's relevance in your project and decide to include or exclude a piece.

Is the roadmap more suitable for particular project types?

This is an end-to-end roadmap designed for new products or services in software development projects. You can, however, use parts of its logic in customization, enhancement, or to revamp projects. The roadmap is not designed for Data Warehousing or Business Intelligence (BI) projects. Now, let's get started!

SECTION II

THE ROADMAP

Phase I: Business Analysis Phase
Pre-Automation Requirements Development

This is a preparatory phase. Pause thinking about the solution requirements, and instead try as much as possible to stay in the present and concentrate on understanding the ground from where you are starting. Your aim is to describe the world where automation will be introduced, the environment and context, the motive behind it, the nature of the people involved, and their needs and challenges. Automation is a powerful enabler with the great potential to support people and organizations, but it shouldn't become "the" goal. Before you begin exploring the automation requirements, you want to understand the real drivers behind the automation and the parameters involved. Without doing so, you will be like a diver diving into water without knowing the nature, depth, and risks.

Why Do We Need this Phase?

Ideally, the Business Analysis phase should precede making any solution scope decision, before contracts are signed with vendors, and requests for proposals are produced. Before contractual boundaries are drawn, it is important to set and align expectations and place the proposed solution into the right context. If you are present during the problem definition phase, this is the right time to explore the items mentioned in this section.

However, if you join the project later after the solution and scope are set, look for evidence that the exercises in this phase have been done. Ask yourself, "Do I have all the information I need to begin the Automation Requirements Development phase? Did anyone answer the questions in this section before me? Is the information documented anywhere? Are stakeholders in agreement on what the problem is and how to solve it?" If the answers to these questions are yes, lucky you! Skip this section and go directly to the next one.

If not, take a step back and run through the exercises in this section first.

For other team members, this may appear as wasted time and unjustified effort. You may have to explain why you need to go through these preparatory exercises. Explain how investing a little time to understand the problem and its context far outweighs the cost of delays that can result from misunderstanding a business need. Highlight the risks inherited in taking a project off from unknown ground. The road ahead may be full of surprises. For example, perhaps the problem was not well defined or the suggested solution does not address the right problem. If so, major requirements changes may occur midway, resulting in overruns, budget strains, and possibly project failure.

Business Analysis does not have to take a long time. Like everything described here, the real point is in the way you think about the issue, not how much time you spend on it.

Now, to the stations in the Business Analysis phase

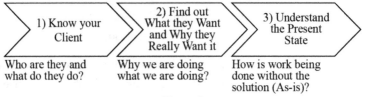

Figure 4

I. Know your Client
Who are they and what do they do?

Exercise Objective: This exercise does not address the project directly. It is a generic exercise to understand the nature and general direction of your client. Knowing your client will help you understand their expectations of you and of the project, their issues and needs, and will help you evaluate the potential risk of conflicts or obstacles.

What to Ask/Look for:
You can simply ask them or anyone who knows them (e.g. the project sponsor) the following questions:
- Who are they?
- What do they do?
- Why are they in business?
- What is their overall vision?

You can also do some research on your own:
- Visit their website
- Read publications written about them or by them
- Ask people who worked with them before
- Ask them to take you on a tour inside the organization

Suggested Analysis Tools: None

Expected Output: Brief description of the organization. No need to document complete details about the client if your audience can find the same information online or elsewhere. Use links and supportive material that your readers can refer to if they wish to learn more.

II. Find out What They Want and Why They Really Want It

Why are we doing what we are doing?

Exercise Objective: You must always ask the question, "What is it that we are trying to achieve and why we are doing what we're doing?" This question sits at the core of your role as an analyst. What is the motivation behind the effort ahead? This is a simple question that in most cases does not take a lot of time, yet it is as essential as planting a seed in the ground to grow a tree. What is it that the client is willing to invest time, effort, and money to achieve? What is the problem? The pain point? Understanding the motive behind the initiative and keeping it in sight is necessary for two reasons: one, you don't want to waste effort producing a solution that fails to meet the original business need; and two, it is important at the beginning of a project to align the expectations of the client with that of the vendor. Both parties must be in agreement as to what can actually be changed and what cannot to avoid conflicts and scope creeps down the road.

What to Ask/Look for: Despite the long list of questions below, they are mostly variations of the same idea. The exercise is not difficult and shouldn't take a long time. Ask:

- Why do you want to change the existing situation?
- Why do you need this solution?
- What are the problems that you want to solve?
- What is wrong with leaving things the way they are?
- If you woke up one day and found yourself working with an ideal solution, what would it look like?
- Is there any other person or party that you think may benefit from this solution?

- What is the error rate in the current situation?

- How difficult it is for you or others to find information?

- How do you feel about the pace of your process as it is now? Is the current way of doing things reasonably efficient and effective?

- Are there any current or future plans in your department, any other department in the organization or even outside the organization, which necessitates the change you want?

Considerations:
- Do not accept motivations at their face value. See if they actually make sense. Motivations that make sense can be:

  - Simplify work processes

  - Reduce processing time

  - Assist employees and their managers in their daily work

  - Reduce the burden of employees' side tasks (i.e., anything that is not the core function of an employee, such as submitting vacation requests)

  - Reach out to more customers

  - Simplify the customer journey

  - Offer more value or options to customers

  - Increase profit or reduce operational costs

  - Basically, whatever helps the organization become more efficient, effective, and responsive

- Watch out for motivations that do not make sense:

  - Complete focus on automation as a target of its own. Some people tend to think that automation alone will solve their problems. Inefficient business processes or lack of employee skills will get in the way of the best automated systems. In fact, in such cases, automation may become a burden rather than an enabler.

- More control. Automation initiatives that only aim to provide more control for managers over employees are tricky initiatives. There is nothing wrong with using automated systems for control purposes, but other benefits may have to be added to ensure a balance. Users must benefit from the systems (or be convinced of their manager's demands) to willingly make the shift to the new system. Otherwise, the system may become a burden, increase the time spent to finish a task or result in data duplication.

- Do not confuse symptoms with problems. Watch out for ready answers and do not take things at face value. People may, for example, attribute delays in responding to customers to a shortage in the workforce, whereas the real reason could be an inefficient filing system where employees waste time in finding a customer file.

- Listen to all levels of the organization and all relevant parties. There are typically three main levels that can be sub-classified as needed: the executive level, the middle management level, and the executor level. Listen to all of the interfacing functions that may directly or indirectly interact with the solution, and those who affect and can be affected by the change. It is important to ensure that all parties understand what can be achieved and what cannot. See if there is an alignment among the different parties' motivations and expectations, and between those and what the new solution can offer.

Suggested Analysis Tools: In many cases, the problem is simple and can be identified and resolved straightaway. There is no need to spend time diving deeper into the underlying causes. A few short interviews and some observation can do the job.

In the more complex projects, however, you might need to use root cause analysis techniques to explore beyond what is seen or said. Complexity in projects may result from different factors:

- High-key projects, such as reforming a public service at a governmental agency

- Projects funded from public budgets or under media scrutiny

- Projects with large investments

- Projects that involve systems with high physical risks, such as machineries and transportation means

In these kinds of projects, you can use additional probing and root cause analysis techniques such as:

- Five Consecutive Whys: Used to probe behind the apparent expressed problems by asking a series of why questions.

- Fish Bones: Helps draw categories of problem areas and then follow the elements in each category for further analysis.

- Mind Maps: Easy to use and play with, and powerful in their ability to analyze and visually show ideas.

> Note 3: Although not necessary, regular projects can also benefit from root cause analysis techniques because they open more discussions and help address issues that the client may not be aware of or overlook.

Expected Output: A vision statement and a list of goals, preferably measurable objectives

III. Understand the Present State

How is work being done without the solution (as-is)?

Exercise Objective: Good analysis mirrors reality and relies on facts. The as-is situation is a foundation brick upon which all remaining work will build. The objective is to "describe" the way work is performed before the introduction of the new solution, not to "analyze" the solution needs.

There are many reasons why this exercise is of immense usefulness for both the effective development of requirements and the overall success of the project:

1. Unlike analysis, which implies a degree of judgment, description is neutral. Understanding what you are actually changing helps you choose the best way to go about that change and develop a pragmatic understanding of what can and cannot be achieved from your current point.

2. The best solution in the world is worthless if it doesn't solve the actual problem or if it is not a good fit for the context in which it operates. Good solutions must factor in the individual conditions of the problem at hand and its specifics. Understanding the present state will enable you to help the solution designers produce what best fits the situation and the people involved in it.

3. You want to learn about what is good and what is not so good about the existing situation. Not all "old" is bad. There must be some good aspects in the existing situation – after all, it is still working in one way or another. Examining the as-is situation helps you determine which parts should be maintained in the new solution, and if not possible, then compensated for by other exceeding benefits. Likewise, it is important to understand the pain points to avoid in the new solution. Otherwise, what is the point in making the change?

4. Users, especially those who haven't gone through the process of implementing IT solutions before, are often at a loss as to how the process works. Sometimes, they are intimidated by the fact that they are expected to answer questions and provide information that they might be held responsible for in the future. Focusing on understanding what they do on a daily basis is a non-threatening task that they can relax and do. It will relieve them from the pressure of making decisions about the solution right away.

5. Going through this exercise will help users organize their thoughts and recognize what they do in a conscious way, which will naturally get them closer to what they expect from a new solution.

6. The as-is description will logically lead to requirements. While they relate the stories of what they do, you will be able to extract needs and details that will fast-forward the following exercises when you reach the Automation Requirements phase. This exercise is a smooth start that opens doors and helps you raise meaningful questions later on.

7. People like to talk about what they do. Giving users this chance will help you build rapport with them, an add-on benefit that you will grow to appreciate as the project moves into more complicated stages.

8. Last but not least, clients tend to appreciate the output of this exercise as a valuable deliverable in its own right. When they see their processes laid out in detail before their eyes, they are better able to analyze their organization efficiency, identify issues, and make improvements (even beyond the scope of the automation project). They may also reuse the deliverable for other purposes, such as initiate other projects, train newcomers, or present one department's work to another.

<u>What to Describe</u>?

Use the following grouping to describe the present state. These three categories form an organization system and constitute the basis of any reform initiative:

- Strategy and processes

- People

- Tooling

The above components are interrelated. Like any system, it is often unrealistic to try to reform one component without the other. For instance, you can't expect to run seamless processes without integrated IT systems (tooling) or well-trained resources who understand the value of their tasks (people). Likewise, the best workforce can't produce good lasting results unless they operate within smart frameworks and be equipped with efficient tools.

What to Ask/Look for per Category:

<u>Overall Strategy and Processes</u>
- What does your typical day at work look like?

- Tell me, what is your role in this workflow?

- What is the most common task you perform?

- What else do you do?

- How do you do that?

- Can I watch you doing it?

- Can I see any documentation that relates to your work?

- Who else performs that task?

- What happens before you do your task?

- Who does what?

- What happens after you are done with that task?

- Who takes over from there and what do they do?

- Can I meet them?

IT Systems

- What operating systems, platforms, and systems are used?

- Can I see the systems you use?

- What do you like about this system, feature, or report?

- What do you not like about this system, feature, or report?

- Is there anything you feel that can be done better or faster?

- How do you organize your files?

- Do you have an archiving system?

- Can I talk to IS to understand the machines and technology used?

People

- Is there an up-to-date organization chart that I can see to understand the structure?

- Who do you report to?

- Who reports to you?

- How many people are on the team?

- How are the teams structured? How many management levels exist? Is the team divided by anything, such as business lines or regions?

- Are there brief job descriptions that I can use to understand the job responsibilities?

- How do you feel about this project?

- Is there anything you feel you need to learn that would better help you with the new work model?

- How can we assist you in this transition?

- What do you need?

- How can we make your task easier?

Observe: Observation is an excellent technique to understand the present state. Watching what people do safeguards against information gaps. Your users may fail to tell you all the details that you need, leave out elements of information that they do not think adds value to your work, or overlook details as givens and do not realize they are omitting them.

Analyze Written Material: Documents analysis is another good way to learn about the business and its operations. Instead of wasting the client's time telling you the full story of the business and its operations, you can consult material such as the organization website, process maps, organization chart, job descriptions, employee handbooks, and manuals to find information.

Suggested Analysis Tools:
- Six Interrogatives: The five Ws and one H questions will help you easily uncover the different aspects of the situation.

- Organization Charts: These will help you:

    - Understand the organization's structure and its efficiency

    - Analyze the users' access privileges (when you reach that point later in the process)

    - Identify relevant stakeholders (a requirements management activity)

- Cross-Functional (Swimlane) Activity Diagrams: If there are processes that require the collaboration of different people, cross-functional activity diagrams are a great tool to visually and simply map them.

- Business Use Cases: For individual tasks and their procedures, use the use cases technique to show the flow of steps and possibly identify inconsistencies between different people's ways of executing the same operations.

- <u>Business Rules, Decision Trees, Decision Tables</u>: List the business rules that govern the business operations and decisions in statements, tables, or charts, depending on the sophistication of the decision-making models.

- <u>Data Dictionary (Skeleton)</u>: This doesn't have to be the complete data dictionary; just list the business entities and the elements they contain. You may also choose to postpone this step until you reach the Automation Requirements Sketching phase.

Expected Output:A descriptive report of the current state categorized by the three dimensions (processes, people, tools). You can also include insights about any inconsistencies, redundancies, bottlenecks, etc.

Depending on the situation, the description may include any of the following:

Category	Possible Output
People	• Organization structure • People roles • People skills • Attitude towards the project
Strategy and Processes	• Business vision • Processes, along with their steps and interfaces with other processes • Glossary of business terminology
Existing Technology	• Hardware • Operating systems • Software applications • Browsers • File storage and archiving systems • Databases • Backup mechanisms • Challenges with existing status

Table 1

Summary

The following table shows a summarized view of the Business Analysis phase exercises. Use it as a cheat sheet.

Objective	Analysis Tools	Expected Output
Know your Client	None	A brief description of the organization
Find out What they Want and Why they Really Want it	Five Whys, Fish Bones, Mind Maps	A vision statement and goals, or preferably measurable objectives
Understand the Present State	Six Interrogatives (Five Ws and one H), Organization Charts, Swimlanes, Business Use Cases, Business Rules, High-Level Data Dictionaries	People: Organization structure, people roles, people skills, attitude towards the project Strategy and Processes: Business vision, processes, along with their steps and interfaces with other processes, glossary of business terminology Technology: Existing hardware (servers and clients), operating systems, software applications, file storage systems and logic, backup mechanisms

Table 2

Phase II: Automation Requirements Development Phase (Core Phase)

You have now reached the core phase of the Requirements Development, where solution specifications are explored. Everything you did in the Business Analysis phase was to prepare the ground for this work.

This phase is divided into two sub-phases: A requirements sketching phase and a requirements detailing phase.

Sub-Phase II.I: Automation Requirements Sketching

Your aim in this phase is to cover the breadth of the solution without diving in depth into any one component. The objective is to capture a distant "helicopter" view of the overall solution and get a picture of the scope of work lying ahead. To achieve this goal, you look at the solution requirements horizontally (rather than vertically), brushing over the full surface, leaving no space uncovered, but without diving into the details of any particular area. The aim is to prepare the groundwork for the solution design and include the main requirements that may cause scope creeps later in the project if not considered in the original design and scope.

Depending on factors such as the size of the project, the needs of the stakeholders, and the project management style, the output from the Requirements Sketching sub-phase can be produced in one self-contained deliverable or combined in a single deliverable with the detailed requirements produced in the subsequent sub-phase. Regardless of the produced deliverables, the Requirements Development effort should still follow the two sub-phase plan.

The following illustration shows the exercises in the requirements sketching phase:

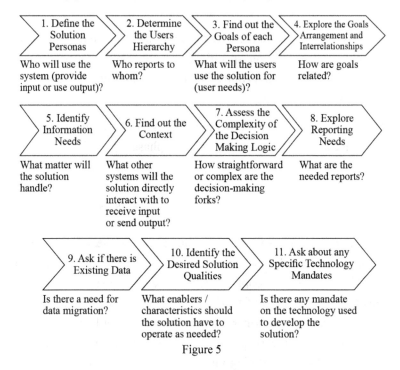

Figure 5

I. Define the Solution Personas

Who will use the system (provide input or use output)?

Exercise Objective: Because systems are mostly operated by human beings (in some cases virtual or hypothetical, such as cars or machines), it is logical to start the conversation by asking who these "operators" are: "Who will use the system?"

What to Ask/Look for: You have probably already identified some potential user groups when you worked on the exercises in the Business Analysis phase. (Remember, each phase prepares for the subsequent one and therefore accelerates it.) For example, as you examined the motive behind the project in Exercise 2: Find out What They Want and Why They Really Want It, you understood (or been told straight out) that managers face certain challenges to fulfill their managerial duties. You may have been told that managers suffer due to the absence of a consolidated source that provides accurate and consistent information. This information should give you a hint that managers are going to be key users of the solution (or at least, information consumers). In fact, the information has already told you about the goals that the managers need from the solution.

Or, while you examined the present state in Exercise 3: Understand the Present State, you may have realized that the front-office and back-office teams collaborate to complete the sales process. You know that these two groups are potential users of the solution, depending on which parts of the process the client decides to automate. Does the client require the front-desk team to use the automated system or will this part of the process remain manual?

Here you can confirm and finalize this information.

> Note 4: The same information may come up repeatedly during discussions in different phases. This information recycling is normal and even encouraged. It helps clients revisit their thoughts and needs, and verify assumptions.

When information that does not belong to the station you are at comes up wrapped in other types of information, do not let them distract you from the objective at hand. Resist the temptation to follow the thread of the information. Do, however, record the pieces that are thrown at you and save them in their relevant buckets (functions, data, business rules, etc) for later. When you reach the station relevant to that specific information, check the information you have, use it as a starting point, and validate, complete, or correct it if needed.

You can use sheets of paper, notebook pages, documents, or presentation slides as buckets to jot down related relevant information for later usage. These buckets typically consist of some information and many questions to validate and clarify in due time.

Ask:

- Who will use the system from the front-end? The direct users who perform actions using the system interface (such as a customer purchasing groceries online).

- Who will use the system from the back-end? Back office users may be:

    - Content management administrators who manage the information users see in the front-end (such as a news editor who uploads or removes news on a news portal).

    - System Administrators concerned with the technical aspect of the system such as diagnosis and performance auditing. Administrators may have different access levels, such as a regular administrator with standard access privileges and a super administrator who enjoys additional privileges.

- Who needs to directly receive information from the system? For example, mobile phone customers receive auto-notifications from Telco company systems through SMSs although they know nothing about these systems.

- Who needs to indirectly receive information from the system? For example, managers may receive reports from the system through other people, such as their assistants, even though they do not directly interact with the system.

- Should the users and their privileges be customizable from the system?

- Is there a possibility user groups will be added or removed in the future?

- What name should each group have?

Notes 5:

1. There is an added value in the exploration of the system administrator role's requirements. It helps you assess the client's flexibility needs. From the required back-end features, you can tell if the client expects a static built-in logic or a highly configurable system.

2. If there are IS and support teams, consult them. The client may be able to tell you some of the back-end features, but these two teams are better able to define system maintenance tasks.

Suggested Analysis Tools: None

Expected Output: A complete User Groups List

Note 6: Possible Variation: Instead of asking about the users first, you can ask the client about the process first and use that as a starting point to learn about the people involved in the process and who among them will use the system.

II. Determine the Users Hierarchy
Who reports to whom?

Exercise Objective: The hierarchical structure of the users is an important point to consider in the design of system architectures. Users' hierarchy affects the granted user privileges to access and manipulate information in the system. How many layers there are in the hierarchy and how flexible this hierarchy is are issues that should be explored early in the project.

What to Ask/Look for: If you already examined the organization chart in Exercise 3: Understand the Present State in the Business Analysis phase, use the information you have as a starting point. If you didn't, it is time to do so now. Ask:
- Who reports to whom?

- How many levels exist in the reporting line?

- Can levels be skipped (for example, a manager can directly access records of employees under his subordinate manager)?

- Is there cross-functional reporting (for example, a manager can see records from employees who report to other managers)?

Suggested Analysis Tools and Expected Output:
- Organization Chart

- (High-level) User Access Privileges Matrix

III. Find out the Goals of each Persona

What will the users use the solution for (user needs)?

Exercise Objective: Users have real life needs. For example, a call center agent needs to record the details of a customer complaint, close a case, or make a payment on behalf of the customer. A citizen needs to renew a driver license, a customer to buy a book, and so forth. Systems are developed to meet the needs of their users. Real life events are the drivers of the system functions. The natural transition from the question "Who will use the system?" is therefore the question "What will they use the system for?"

Once again, you probably already have a good starting point from the exercises you went through in the Business Analysis phase. Here, you complete the information you have.

What to Ask/Look for:

- When will you use the system?

- What do you want to achieve from the solution?

- What parts of your existing work should be automated?

Your focus here is on the "what" not the "how" of the function. Don't worry yet about the detailed steps to achieve the goal. Define the goal, the end result or the outcome, not the steps that lead to them. Remember, you are hovering over the solution from a distance. Do, however, apply some analysis to evaluate the complexity that may lie behind the goals. Check the as-is procedures output from Exercise 3: Understand the Present State in the Business Analysis phase to get an indication of the complexity involved in achieving the goal and the level of automation needed.

Suggested Analysis Tools:

- <u>User Stories</u>: Borrowed from the Agile Methodology, user stories are a powerful tool to collect user goals. Putting goals on spread out cards helps identify missing goals, rethink unnecessary goals, find associations between goals, spot shared components among user groups, remove redundancies, and prioritize needs.

- Use Case Diagrams: Use Case Diagrams are a more traditional technique to list user goals. They give a coherent visual presentation of the user goals, their order, and relationships (relationships among goals is the focus of the next exercise).

Expected Output: The output of this exercise completes the User Profiles List produced from the previous exercise. It can be:

- User Goals Lists
- Use Case Diagrams
- User Stories (if you work in an Agile project)

> Note 7: Both User Stories and Use Case Diagrams have their own strengths. With their segregated cards, User Stories help users think better and allow for freer brainstorming in elicitation and analysis. Use Case Diagrams, on the other hand, are good for requirements communication because they link the goals together in a coherent picture.

IV. Explore the Goals Arrangement and Interrelationships

How are goals related?

Exercise Objective: What you have now is a list of objectives, and unless you used Use Case Diagrams in the last exercise, the list probably still needs arrangement and linking to be complete and form a basis for an integrated solution. Examining the interrelationships between the goals is an important activity to analyze the intra-operability between the system functions and safeguard against architecture flaws.

What to Ask/Look for:

- How do goals impact each other?

- Are there goals (of the same or different users) that complete each other or could fall under a parent goal? For example: Browsing items and paying online can be standalone goals in their own merit or grouped under a bigger goal "Place an Order."

- Could completing a goal trigger another one? For example: Completing the last step of the employee reallocation process in the HR system could trigger an order to the Logistics department's online system to issue the employee stationeries and laptop.

- Could achieving a goal cancel another one? For example: A change of address may result in the cancellation of a voting card in the first location.

- Could a goal override another one? For example: A special loan agreement with the bank could override the issuance of a standard loan.

- Could a goal reverse another one? For example: Returning an item would reverse the addition of a customer reward points that were added after the item purchase.

- Are there any goals shared by more than one user/group?

- Are there goals that are prerequisites (could also be an include relationship) to other goals? For example: A student must register to attend a Master Thesis seminar before they can choose the thesis topic.

- Could a goal extend to another one? For example: Apply for a college, and then apply for a specific department within the college.

Keep an eye on the objectives classification and grouping. One objective may be a main function with multiple sub-functions and UI screens in the system. For example, Buy an Add-on Service Online would result in child functions such as Select Service, Place in Shopping Cart, Pay, and Receive Confirmation.
On the other hand, another objective may become one field on a screen (at least from the user's perspective). For example, Track the Sales Rep Name on Invoices is a field on the Invoice entity, or Track If the User Wants to Receive Promotions may be a checkbox.

> Note 8: While this is not the time to decide how a requirement will be implemented, it is important to group the objectives in a meaningful way. For example, put everything related to Pay Invoice under one section title. Avoid dragging lists where requirements are listed one after the other without a structure. Use titles to categorize the list; the more structure you use, the easier it will be to read, design, and manage the requirements.

Suggested Analysis Tools and Expected Output:
- System Structure Breakdown (also called Functional Decomposition): One of the best tools you can use to show the

anatomy and organization of a system's functions.

- <u>Use Case Diagrams</u>: If you haven't already produced Use Case Diagrams in the last exercise, you can do so here after you have examined the links between the user goals. The diagram will give you a good visual representation of the user goals order, missing goals, unnecessary goals, and redundancies among user groups

V. Identify Information Needs
What matter will the solution handle?

Exercise Objective: Operations, processes, transactions, reports, and systems are all designed to handle information. Giving special attention targeted to the information handled by a solution is essential to see the full picture. Thinking from a functional processing perspective only is likely to leave gaps in the requirements. When you don't examine the matter being manipulated by those functions, you risk missing important aspects. For example, in a customer profile management function, examining the elements that the profile is composed of and the validations ran on them can give you great insights – possibly more than you do when you think about the functions of add, update, or delete.

What to Ask/Look for: The best approach to address this exercise is to examine the client's documentation, such as the application forms they use, customer records, invoices, bills, complaint forms, etc. You can extract information from this material and validate it with the users in interviews. Ask:

- Which information do you process?

- What information do you need to process this?

- Where do you get the information from?

- How different does this information become after processing?

- What is the volume of records you get per unit of time (hour, day, week, etc.)?

- Do you keep this information?

- Where do you keep it?

- Do you archive the information? Where? For how long?

Note 9: You already have a starting point from Exercise 3: Understand the Present State in the Business Analysis Phase. Use this material to decide which information requires handling by the system and which doesn't, and if there is a need to change the existing information structures. It is possible that the client wishes to use the automation initiative as an opportunity to make changes in the data they capture (for example, remove unused elements or add new ones).

Suggested Analysis Tools and Expected Output:

- Data Dictionaries Skeleton: List the entities that should be handled by the solution along with the elements they include. Don't go into the configuration details of each element (field) such as the field length and type. This detailing will be done in the Requirements Detailing phase.

- Entity Relationship Diagrams: ERDs offer a good visual representation of the relationship among the entities of a solution. If the Data Dictionaries Skeleton shows the anatomy of each entity separately, the ERDs will show the complete intra-related structure of the information entities.

VI. Find out the Context

What other systems will the solution directly interact with to receive input or send output?

Exercise Objective: In the previous exercises, your focus has been on the inner physiology of the system. But systems, like everything else, do not operate in vacuums. They relate to other systems, automated or manual. You have possibly identified the manual systems when you analyzed the direct and indirect users of the systems. Here, you complete the task and examine the integration with external automated systems. Integration is a major component that needs planning and accurate estimation from the solution team, and therefore must be explored early in the process.

What to Ask/Look for: It is possible you already found out about at least some of the integration requirements when you explored the user goals in Exercise 2: Find out the Goals of Each User Group. Use the information you have to guide your search for the integration requirements. Ask:
- What data, messages, or calls should the system send to other systems?
- What data, messages, or calls should the system receive from other systems?
- Which format will the exchanged data be in?
- At what specific event or time will the exchange occur?
- How frequently will the exchange take place?
- What is the volume of the exchanged data?

Suggested Analysis Tools and Expected Output:
- Context Diagram
- Requirement Statements

VII. Assess the Complexity of the Decision-Making Logic

How straightforward or complex are the decision-making forks?

Exercise Objective: Business rules definition is generally a detailed analysis step. At this stage, the aim is not to fully discover or analyze all the business rules permutations, but rather to assess the implied complexity of their logic. This exercise is particularly important in projects that deal with business operations that rely on particularly complex decision making, such as:

- Insurance eligibility and claims reimbursement processing

- Financial loans and investment

- Public social benefits or legal permits eligibility processing

Such operations usually rely on relatively complex logic to process data and deduce accurate results and conclusions. The structure of the process itself may not be so complex, but the involved decision points and the resulting branching out could be. In this type of work, business rules sit at the core of the business activity and its automation, and it's important to assess the amount of work required to implement them.

What to Ask/Look for: Use the information you already collected from Exercise 3: Understand the Present State in the Business Analysis phase, and ask:

- When do you have to make a decision? At which points?

- How frequently are decisions made?

- How many branches split out from a decision-making point?

- What are the constraints that may prevent you from completing a task? You can use the goals collected in Exercise 2: Find out the Goals of Each User Group to guide the discussion about constraints by focusing on the constraints of one function at a time.

- What criteria do you apply to make a decision? How many are there per decision?

- How frequently do decision criteria change? In some un-structured (or semi-structured) environments, complexity often results from the changes to the decision criteria rather than the criteria themselves. For example, frequent changes to the rules or its exceptions may result in contradictory sets of confusing rules, which become challenging to standard-ize. The best way to handle them may be to provide a feature that allows users to define and configure rules on their own to allow flexibility and ease of maintenance.

After asking these questions, read the client's documentation. Ex-amine the application forms such as reimbursement claims, regis-tration forms, permit requests, loan applications, or the organiza-tion policies and rules.

Suggested Analysis Tools:

- Business Rules Classification

- Decision Trees

- Decision Tables

Expected Output: A rough estimation of the amount of applied rules and an example of a set of rules that has an average complex-ity – or maximum complexity – presented as:

- Requirement Statements

- Incomplete Decision Trees drafts

- Incomplete Decision Tables drafts

VIII. Explore Reporting Needs
What are the needed reports?

Exercise Objective: No one wants to scope a project with the assumption that there is a need to produce four reports, only to realize later that there are in fact seventeen, or to realize that the reports data is not captured anywhere in the system. You need to know the number of required reports and get a brief understanding of the information they contain to ensure the system captures or derives it somewhere.

What to Ask/Look for:
- Why do you need the report?
- Whow will have access to it?
- Which information should be included in this report?
- Do you want it generated automatically at certain times?
- If yes, which times? Where should be placed? Should the system send you a notification?
- How will you filter the report data?
- Do you need grouping? Average? Sums?
- Do you need graphs?

Suggested Analysis Tools: None

Expected Output: A brief high-level list of the required reports that contains the report name, purpose, and brief description of its usage and content

IX. Ask if there is Existing Data
Is there a need for data migration?

Exercise Objective: If the client has been running other systems to manage their operations, it is likely that they will need the data in those systems to be transferred to the new solution, especially if the new system provides features that rely on historical data such as trends comparison reports between different years. The data stored in legacy systems carry the history of the business operation, and therefore, data migration is often a fundamental element to ensure continuity of the business operations.

All the details related to data migration are outlined in the Transitional Requirements Phase section. At this stage, there is no need to go through all the details; only indicate if there will be a need for data migration and the likely related complexity. Migration complexity may be due to factors such as:

1. The number of data sources and the format consistency of those sources.
2. The data consistency and integrity and the effort needed to identify duplicates and inaccuracies, or perform data cleansing; for example, numerical fields that contain user notes or special characters.

For What to Ask/Look for, Suggested Analysis Tools, and Expected Output, see the Transitional Requirements section.

X. Identify the Desired Solution Qualities

What enablers/characteristics should the solution have to operate as needed?

Exercise Objective: The solution qualities (commonly known as non-functional requirements) such as security, reliability, performance, accuracy, and so forth are major differentiators between first-rate systems and poor ones. A solution is not solely judged on the functions it offers, but also on the quality of those functions. All cars move (function), but not all cars are the same. The real differentiators in cars are quality features like speed, safety and comfort features, and all the other qualities that make a race car stand out from an ordinary passenger car.

What to Ask/Look for: Ideally, you should agree on the qualities that the solution should have as early as possible – preferably during the contract or proposal preparation. At the least, the following major qualities should be explored early because they significantly affect the scope of work:

- Security
- Capacity
- Performance
- Availability (especially in hosted applications)

Details of all qualities are listed in the next section, Requirements Detailing phase. Here, I only list some points that could have significant impact on the scope of work, and should therefore get a high-level examination at this stage:

Quality	Questions
Capacity	▪ Is there a rough estimate of the present and future number of users? ▪ If not, what is the limit that can be reached with the available resources? ▪ What is the maximum number of users who are likely to access the system or a particular function at the same time?
Accessibility	▪ Where are the users located? ▪ How will they be connected? ▪ Are there special accessibility requirements (such as voice recognition)?
Security	▪ Are there any sensitive data that requires protection? ▪ If yes, what is the protection required for it? Manipulation of data or just viewing? ▪ Should connections be secure?
Performance	Are there any specific concerns about the processing speed?
Accuracy	In certain situations, such as voice recognition systems, what is an acceptable error rate?
Stability and Reliability	In certain situations, such as hosted services, what is an acceptable failure rate?
Recoverability	What is the expected recovering mechanism if an error occurs?
Processing timing	Should transactions be handled real-time or in batches? This is particularly important in integration.
Availability	What are the acceptable unavailability frequency and the tolerated down time?
Flexibility	Are there special configuration requirements of the system administrator or super user?

Table 3

Suggested Analysis Tools: Many qualities require technical and infrastructure knowledge that an analyst may or may not have. Other solution team members can provide details of the qualities implementation. This is how the analyst can assist them:

1. Find out the client concerns from a problem standpoint. For example, the client's priority to handle heavy traffic on a particular function at a specific time of the day.
2. Bring those concerns to the technical team for consideration and discussion.
3. Take the proposed solution alternatives back to the client (you can ask the solution team to join the discussion with the client) and ensure that the suggested solutions meet the client's needs.

Expected Output: Requirement Statements

XI. Ask about any Specific Technology Mandates

Is there any mandate on the technology used to develop the solution?

Exercise Objective: If there is a need to use a particular technology or tool to develop the solution, it is important to learn about that at this phase to allow for reasonable planning and to set expectations. For example, maybe the customer IT department can support and maintain applications developed using only certain technologies or perhaps they have certain tool licenses that they need to use.

Summary

The following table shows a summarized view of the Automation Requirements Sketching phase exercises. Use it as a cheat sheet.

Objective	Analysis Tools	Expected Output
Define the Solution Personas	None	User Groups list
Determine the Users Hierarchy	Organization Chart, User Access Privileges Matrix	Organization Chart, User Access Privileges Matrix
Find out the Goals of each Persona	Use Case Diagrams, System Structure Breakdown, System Thin Slice	Use Case Diagrams, User Stories, User Profiles and Goals List
Explore the Goals Arrangement and Interrelationships	Use Case Diagrams, System Structure Breakdown, System Thin Slice	Use Case Diagrams, System Structure Breakdown, System Thin Slice
Identify Information Needs	Data Dictionary, ERD	Data Dictionary Skeleton, ERD
Find out the Context	Context Diagram	Context Diagram, Requirement Statements
Assess the Complexity of the Decision- Making Logic	Business Rules, Decision Trees, Decision Tables	Requirement statements, Incomplete Decision Trees drafts, Incomplete Decision Tables drafts
Explore the Reporting Needs	None	Reports List
Ask if there is Existing Data	None	Requirements statements and tables
Identify the esired Solution Qualities	None	Requirement Statements
Ask about any Specific Technology Mandates	Questions	Statements

Table 4

Sub-Phase II.II: Automation Requirements Detailing

In the previous phase, you produced a set of structured stakeholder requests that express user[3] intentions, needs, and requests described in a mostly logical form. For the most part, there was no mandate on any specific design or physical implementation options. To a great extent, you operated within the problem domain. Here, you turn your focus to the solution domain to produce the solution design specifications.

The following table shows the switch between the two phases:

Sketching Phase	Detailing Phase
More focus on the problem	More focus on the solution
Abstract logical requests	Concrete physical specifications
Requirements open for different implementation options	Specific Implemental solution design

Table 5

The solution design you are going to work on here includes all parts of the design of interest to the involved stakeholders. They can be the solution behavior, the solution interface, the user experience, the business rules, and the flow of events. The solution design specification is commonly known as functional design and it covers the gap between the stakeholders' logical needs and the technical implementation requirements. In some cases, however, this part of the design may extend to internal system workings specifications such as integration with other systems and logical data models (sometimes even physical models). The decision to include these parts depends on the question: What is of interest to the project stakeholders?

---

3 The word User is used here in the broader sense; it includes any stakeholder who has a say in the requirements whether they directly use the system or not

Technical designers must be involved to validate the technical feasibility and provide insight on implementation possibilities or limitations. It is important that this exercise does not turn into a technical matter. Decisions that affect the experience of the solution consumers (for example, those who use, maintain, or monitor the solution) must be made in agreement with them.

The following are the stations in the Requirements Detailing phase in order:

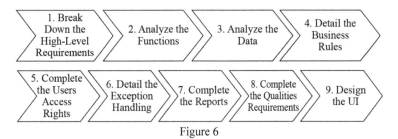

Figure 6

I. Break Down the High-Level Requirements

Exercise Objective: Think of the high-level requirements you have from the previous phase as compositions of units that should be defragmented to gain a deeper understanding of the requirements to reveal their bits and pieces. This exercise breaks the requirements to pieces. It takes little time and produces great value, as it leaves no sides of the requirements unexamined. It is just the beginning of the close-up analysis. The next exercises will also offer a deeper insight into the requirements.

> Note 10: Each high-level requirement will typically expand to a number of detailed system design specification requirements. A high-level requirement stated in one line may expand to children requirements that fill lines or even pages.

What to Ask/Look for: Use the six famous questions in the Six Interrogatives technique: why, what, who, where, when, and how.

You can use the list of questions I am suggesting here as a starting point. But keep in mind that the exact questions you will come up with every time greatly depend on the particular requirement at hand. Some questions will prove more relevant to a particular requirement than other questions. For example, a requirement that says "Solution shall allow users to record customer complaints" warrants questions like: Who are those users? How long should the system keep this information? Which data should be recorded? Whereas, a requirement that states "Solution shall allow users to cancel a customer complaints" may call for different questions. What happens when a complaint is cancelled (should it be stored or completely purged)? When can users do that? Who cannot do that?

Depending on the situation, some questions will produce superficial answers and some may surprise you with the level of details that they reveal. For example, in some cases the where or the when would generate more information than the who and the what, or vice versa. It is important, however, to experiment with all six questions before making a judgment about their relevancy. Think about all the questions carefully before you decide what is not applicable. Consider it a game; you are, in a way, toying around with the information to reach as far and as deep as you can. That said, pay careful attention. Avoid going with easy answers and rushing to conclusions. Answers may repeat information or appear to shed little light on the requirement. When that happens, take a second look before you move on.

Work done in previous phases is likely to provide answers to some of the questions. I recommend you still go through all questions to validate the information and complete any points that were possibly missed.

Here is how you can use this tool.

Why

You have already examined the "why" when you analyzed the rationale behind the project. Here you zoom in and focus on specific requirements to ensure they have a valid justification and meaningful value. For example:

- Why do we need this feature?

- Why do we need to do it in that way?

- If we are redoing the as-is, what is the value in keeping things the way they are?

- If we are changing the as-is, why are we doing so? What is the value?

Who

The "who" question is particularly interesting. To get the best results, ask the question in both the affirmative and negative modes.

For example, who can perform a certain task and who can't. There is a great benefit in doing so. Many users will remember to answer the questions in an affirmative mode (who is the producer or the consumer of an action), but may forget to mention who is not until they are required to explicitly reflect on it. Try the following:

Who

- Who will use this function? Who should not use it?

- Who is impacted by it? Who is not?

- Who will provide input? Who will not?

- Who will receive output? Who will not?

- Who should know about the function? Who should not?

What

- What is requested?

- What is really needed beyond what is requested?

- What is happening now?

- What can we do? What can't we do?

Where

- Where will the system/function be physically deployed and used (country, region, office, or home)?

- Where in the process should an activity or a check take place (before or after a certain point)?

- Where will it appear for the user (for example, in the screens flow)?

- Where will data be stored, sent, or placed?

When

- When will the function be useful?

- When should the feature be delivered (in comparison to other functions)?

How
- How will the option be implemented?
- How should we setup the software and hardware to fulfill the requirement?

> Note 11: The difference between how and what is often blurry. To distinguish between them, think of "what" as what needs to be done or thought of at that specific time in the project, whereas the "how" is the part that team members will think of at the subsequent phases. You can think of the "what" as the level of detail you should provide as an input to the next phase.

Suggested Analysis Tools: The Six Interrogatives (also known as the five Ws and one H) – the why, what, who, where, when, and how – are your best dissection tool to make the transition from high-level requirements to the detailed system specifications.

Expected Output: The output of this exercise is not a deliverable in itself, but rather a list of questions and pieces of information that should be taken to the client or to the solution building team for further elaboration and investigation. I recommend that you run this exercise on your own first and come up with a list of questions before you seek answers from others.

II. Analyze the Functions

Exercise Objective: Functions are the nucleus components of software systems. In this step, you detail the logic of each function in the system.

Before we go through the details of the functions analysis process, we must first agree on a definition of a function from an analytical perspective. The function we are concerned with here is an action (or series of actions) performed by the system to achieve a goal that serves a user or a business objective. In a typical function, the system receives input (information or choices) from the user or another function. The system then processes this information, and produces an output that may or may not be displayed to the user. Functions in that sense includes two components: A visible (evident) part and an internal (hidden) part[4]:

- Users can see and interact with the visible (evident) part, also called functional view.

- Users do not interact with the invisible (hidden) part. This is the internal processing part where the system runs its "magic" to process the input and produce the desired results.

The two keywords in this separation are "User Interaction" and "Internal Processing".

Why is this separation important? When you analyze and document functional requirements, you have to differentiate between what the users are interested in and what not. Mostly, users will care about their experience and the results they get. In this case, you only describe the external view of the function; there is no need to confuse your audience with irrelevant details of no interest to them. In some cases, however, you will find users who want to know more about the way the solution is designed, including parts

---

4 The concept of evident and hidden is taken from the book "Exploring Requirements, Quality Before Design, Donald Gause and Gerald Weinberg, 1989"

beyond their immediate experience. In this case, you can show the other invisible part.

Here is another reason why it is useful to consider this distinction when you work with functions. The same function (same internal processing logic) can be invoked by users or by background events without user's intervention. Analytically, in this case, the difference is in the channel or the trigger point, and possibly also the output direction (for example, displayed to the user or not). But it remains one function.

What to Ask/Look for: Functions are best analyzed using analysis tools (see the Suggested Analysis Tools below). The following are a few questions that you can use to initiate discussions[5]:

- What are the steps in performing the function?
- Is there a specific order of steps that must be followed?
- Are there any constraints that could change the way the function handles data?
- What is the input of the function? External and internal data or order input?
- What is the output? External and internal data or result output?

Suggested Analysis Tools: Many tools can be used to analyze functions. Some analysis tools are better suited to analyze the visible part of the function, while other ones are more suitable for the analysis of the internal processing part. Some are a good fit for both. Consider the following:

- <u>Six Interrogatives</u>: The six interrogatives are one of the most effective tools to initiate the analysis of a particular function. They're good discussion openers. If you have not already

---

5 The same questions are listed in Method H, see the Tools section

used them in the previous exercise to dissect the function requirement, I advise you to do so here. You can use them to analyze the complete function including the evident and hidden parts.

- Use Cases: Use Cases are the best tool to analyze the user interaction part of a function. Use it only for the evident part of the function.

- Method H: Method H is a strong tool that can help you inspect the tiny details of how the system processes a function. You can use it to analyze the internal processing part only or the full function beginning to end, including the evident and hidden parts.

- Flowcharts: Flowcharts have a wealth of notations that make them suitable to analyze and describe internal processing and communicate them to the solution team. Be careful, though, if you use them with users, as they may seem confusing to the not-so-IT-savvy. You can use them to describe the internal processing (and complement them with use cases to describe the evident part) or to describe the full function, including both the evident and hidden parts.

- Interaction Diagrams: You can use them to show the function steps instead of use cases. Interaction Diagrams are simpler than flowcharts and therefore are easier to understand.

Expected Output: Depending on the situation, the output can be a bundle of any of the following: requirement statements, use cases, flowcharts, interaction diagrams, or procedures textual description.

III. Analyze the Data

Exercise Objective: Software applications are first and foremost "information" systems. Processing data is their primary purpose regardless of the specific nature of the application or the data. In the traditional Structured Systems Analysis and Design methodology, the separation between functions and data is a foundational concept and remains one of its main useful analytical principles. Regardless of the applied analysis methodology, data remains a core focus of information systems and should therefore be given proper attention and analyzed separately from the logic of the functions, methods, or operations. Whether the information is to eventually be presented in the design in the form of relational data models defining data entities and elements, or in the form of UML models defining classes and objects, the essence is pretty much the same from a data analysis perspective. There are important details that can be discovered only when special attention is given to the data. Thinking only about functions is like designing a processor without understanding the material it processes.

What to Ask/Look for: You have already produced a data dictionary skeleton in Exercise 4: Identify Information Needs in the Requirements Sketching phase. Here is the time to pull it out and complete the details of each data entity, element, and flow.
Explore the following checks for each data element/field in each entity:

- Label: The name that should be given to the element or field (should be a familiar name used by the business/users).

- Input: What is the source of the element value?

- Will the user manually enter a value – simple input?

- Will the system automatically populate the element from stored values? For example, user enters customer data through the Add Customer function and the system automatically displays it in the Add Invoice function.

- Will the system generate the value from an internal process such as automatic calculation?

- Does the data come from another system?

- Field Type: What is the field type suitable for the field (text – list of values – free form – numeric – alphanumeric)? If you are not sure of the type, indicate the exact expected values and the designers will decide the best-suited type.

- Length: Plan the length based on the longest value the element may hold, and depending on the situation, indicate potential expansion to accommodate possible future changes.

- Mandatory: Is the element mandatory and must be filled before the record is saved or processed (for example, submitted or sent).

- Unique: Or can it be repeated?

- Updateable: Can a user update the value in the field (whether it has been manually entered or auto-populated)?

- Displayed: Should the element be displayed to the user or remain hidden (such as keys)?

- Auto-incrementing: If the element holds numbers, should it auto-increment? If yes, by how many digits (1, pairs, 10s, etc.)?

- Logical Validations/Business Rules: Are there any special rules that control the field? For example, does it accept zeros? Is there a range that cannot be exceeded? Must the value follow a certain business rule?

- Syntax Validations: Should the value entered in the field be structured in a certain format?

- Dependency: Does the field depend on the value entered in another field or through another screen? For example, the list of possible values in the Employees field may be filtered based on the selected value in the Unit field, or the allowed value changes based on another element (for example, the allowed numbers change based on the credit card type).

- Default Value: Is there an expected default value? If yes, what is it and where does it come from?

- If the field has a list of values: What are the possible values?

- If the field is an amount: Should the currency be displayed? If yes, should it be a prefix or suffix?

- If the field is a date:

  - Is it Gregorian, Lunar, or Hindu?

  - Should it be written in letters (Jan 2011) or numerals (01/2011)?

  - How should the date components be ordered (day, month, year; month, day, year; or some other way)?

  - What is the field length (00-00-0000; 00-00-00; 0-0-00; or something else)?

  - What about separators (dashes, slashes, spaces)?

Suggested Analysis Tools: To analyze the details of the data, you have to look at it from two points of view:

- Its static nature (what is each entity composed of and how is each element configured)

- Its dynamic nature (how data flows in the system)

The following are the tools that you can use to analyze the two views of data:

Static View

- <u>Data Dictionaries:</u> help you define the configuration of each data element (although the data flow component of data dictionaries belongs to the dynamic view, data dictionaries are still mentioned in the static view because the other three components are static)

- <u>Entity Relationship Diagrams</u>: present the relationships between different data entities

- <u>Class Diagrams</u>: Same as ERD

Dynamic View

- <u>Data Flow Diagrams</u>: Help you further understand how the system is expected to handle and move data

- <u>State Diagrams</u>: Show how a data object moves from one state to another throughout its lifecycle

Expected output:

- A detailed data dictionary (typically presented in tables)

- Entity Relationships Diagrams

- Class Diagrams

- State Diagrams

- Requirement Statements

IV. Detail the Business Rules

Exercise Objective: By the time you reach this stop, you have undoubtedly already discovered many business rules. Business rules in specific are typically mentioned in the context of other information when users explain processes, procedural scenarios, or data validations. For example, users may have already told you that the application process for an insurance policy go through different levels of verifications, the first of which is the customer's location coverage. They may have touched on that when they described the overall Policy Eligibility process or when they described what they personally do to verify application.

Additionally, the analysis tools that you used in the previous stops (particularly Method H) should have helped you to classify the business rules. For example, when you analyzed the verification function in Exercise 2: Analyze the Functions, you touched on the involved business rules such as the constraint to submit only one request at a time. Or perhaps you learned that the policy amount cannot exceed a specific limit when you examined the data elements in the Exercise 3: Analyze the Data.

But if this is so, what is the point of dedicating a special stop for business rules? The fact that business rules are mentioned in the context of other types of information makes them subject to being overseen. Even if you paid good attention in the previous exercises and extracted business rules that were wrapped in other information, your users may have forgotten to mention some rules. For example, they may have said how the process moved if the answer to a decision is yes, but forgot to mention the alternative route if the answer is no; or fail to consider certain situations where they apply informal rules (such as to direct a case to their supervisors when they do not know how to handle it). To avoid pitfalls like these, we dedicate a special stop for business rules so that both the analyst and the users can stop and examine their lists of business rules and complete or correct them if necessary.

What to Ask/Look for:

- What criteria are used to make a certain decision?

- Does the order of decisions make a difference?

- How often do these decisions take place?

- How often do the decision criteria change?

- How often do people override formal decisions? Under what conditions does that happen and who authorizes the overriding?

- Did we list all the business rules? Are all forks identified (for example, what if the answer to a question is yes and what if it is no)?

- Do we need to add more business rules?

- Are there any situations when users make decisions without realizing they are business rules? Should these decisions be formalized?

- Can any of the listed rules be standardized and used in different processes and functions?

- Are our business rules flexible enough to respond to business changes?

- Do we have rules that govern how to react if a certain business rule is violated?

- Would it help to document the business rules in a decision-making model?

Suggested Analysis Tools:

- Business Rules: The simplest way to complete decisions is to apply the four categorizations of business rules (See the Tools section).

- Decision Trees: You can use Decision Trees in complex decision making logic where the chronological order of the decisions matter.

- Decision Tables: You can use Decision Tables in complex decision-making logic where the chronological order of the decisions does not matter.

Expected Output: Textual Business Rules Statements, Decision Trees, and Decision Tables.

V. Complete the Users Access Rights

Exercise Objective: Users Access Rights can be part of the Business Rules. It is, however, separated in a station of its own to make sure they are given careful attention. Here, you specify each role's access rights to data entities and system functions. If the rights are to be user customizable, identify the groups and the possible rights.

What to Ask/Look for:
- Who can view this? Who cannot?

- Who can add, change, or delete? Who cannot?

- Can rights be delegated?

- Is there a case where rights are automatically suspended for any reason?

Suggested Analysis Tools: Access Rights Matrix

Expected Output: Access Rights can be documented as:
- A matrix that shows the map of roles to entities, data subsets, screens, functions, or reports

- Business rules on specific data fields inside the Data Dictionary

- Business rules statements

VI. Detail the Exception Handling

Exercise Objective: Analyzing business rules naturally leads to the consideration of the handling of exceptional cases. Smart systems and processes are typically built to serve the common most frequently occurring cases, not based on exceptions. For example, you would not impose a complete prohibition on the access of a piece of data because there is a potential for fraud, or forbid people from crossing a street because a few would do so when the light is red. Systems should cater to the common cases first. They should, however, have rules in place to handle exceptions.

Considering exceptions is an important factor in judging how smart a system or process is. Systems and processes must be flexible enough to be able to handle exceptions, should the need arise. Handling exceptions means that the process is not halted, but does not mean permitting what should not be permitted. For example, reasonable control points should be put in place to protect sensitive data. Balancing between ease of operation for the authorized user and inaccessibility for the unauthorized must be considered to ensure both needs are reasonably met.

Exceptions can be any of the following:
- Things that go wrong, like a crashed system or a broken street light
- Rare cases different from the average occurring cases. For example, a client record with an unusual name or address format
- Unusual or unexpected use of the system or manipulation of data. For example, attaching a file in an incompatible format

What to Ask/Look for:
- What could go wrong?
- What could be different from the standard setup?

- How should the system respond to special cases?
- How can you report a special case and learn from it for future cases?

The best people to refer to in order to identify exception handling cases are:
- The users: Users know when they weren't able to apply the standard rules due to problems, mistakes, or special situations.
- Their managers: They know the uncommon cases where their subordinates needed guidance and special decisions.
- The testers: Testers are pretty good in finding problems in systems, which makes them the best candidates to brainstorm potential issues.

You can also brainstorm with the solution delivery team and review error logs from older systems or customer complaints for ideas.

Suggested Analysis Tools: None

Expected Output: Textual statements listed in any of the following ways:
- Within requirements related to a particular function
- Under a separate section for Exception Handling
- In the Business Rules section

Most likely, exception handling will result in the identification of error or warning messages. For each message, include:
- What is wrong or uncommon?
- Why is it wrong or uncommon?
- How will the system handle it?
- What should the user do to proceed beyond the exception point – such as correcting a value or referring to the system administrator or senior staff?

VII. Complete the Reports

Exercise Objective: In the Requirements Sketching phase, you constructed the reports' skeletons by identifying each report name, description, and purpose. Here, you detail the reports' content and design.

What to Ask/Look for: For each report, address the following. The information you are looking for belongs to three categories.

- Report metadata
- Report filtering
- Report content: Report header, body, and footer

Report Metadata

- Description: Why do users need this report?
- Distribution Method: Will the report be printed? Will it be automatically generated and emailed to users? Will a notification be sent or the report stored in a certain location?
- Specific Output/Export Format: PDF, Excel, other format?
- Report Usage Frequency: Daily, weekly, monthly, or yearly?
- Exception Handling: How will the system respond if the user runs a report that does not contain data? What if the report takes a long time to generate?
- Dimensions: Is this a one-dimensional or a multi-dimensional report?
- Access Rights: Who has access to the report?
- Currencies: Should the report show amounts in different currencies?
- Is there a need for charts?

Report Filtering

- What search criteria will the user use to limit the report data?

- How will these criteria be ordered on the search criteria screen?
- If an error occurs in filtering, which message will be displayed? (Example: Record does not exist.)

Report Header
- What information should you include in the report header, if any? Username, Date and Time, Report Title, Page Number, Logo?

Report Body
- Columns: What data elements does each column read from?
- Sorting: Which column(s) of the report columns will be used to sort data?
- Grouping rules: How will records be grouped? Will they be grouped by department, then employee title, or vice versa?
- Calculations: What are the formulas used to produce any data in the report, if any?
- In case of hierarchical elements (such as in financial statements), how will the hierarchy look like?

Report Footer
- Sum: Should the report provide subtotals? Grand total?
- Average: Should the report provide averages for any values in the report?
- Informational data such as page number, company name.

Suggested Analysis Tools: None

Expected Output: Detailed Reports design specifications, usually in a table format or as a prototype

VIII. Complete the Qualities Requirements

Exercise Objective: Time to explore the non-functional requirements (system qualities)!

What to Ask/Look for: Depending on the information you have from the high-level quality requirements exercise in the last phase, check if the following points have been covered:

Integration
If your solution interfaces with other systems, think of the following, where applicable:
- What event will initiate the connection (time-based or activity-based)?
- What data elements will be exchanged? In what format?
- Which APIs, Web Services, or Protocols will be used?
- Will the system write in another system database? What is the data model?

Exception handling
- What happens if the connection times out during data exchange?
- What happens if the data exchanged is invalid?

Logging Requirements
- Is the system required to keep a history log of certain activities?
- What exactly should be logged (specific activities and elements)?
- Is there any particular format requirements?
- Where should the log be stored?
- When should logging take place (real time, daily, etc.)?

Capacity and Performance

- How many users will use the system?

- How many times will a particular transaction be performed per unit of time? For example, ten bidding hits per minute.

- How many records will be stored in the database of the main business entities (such as the Customers table)?

- Is there a potential growth of stored records or system users in the coming years? If so, what is it? For example, if the customer has plans to expand the market or introduce promotional events, this may cause an increase in the number of users/records. Growth rate can be presented as a percentage per period of time (for example, 20% increase in the coming five years).

- How many users will concurrently use the system? Plan for the maximum probability.

- How long does it take to reach the peak traffic on a certain function? How long does it stay at peak? (Example: 1,000 transactions reached after three hours of operation and remains so for one hour.)

- What is the acceptable system response time (for example, five seconds)?

- What is the pages hit ratio (which pages are more likely to be used by the users)?

- How much of the machine resources will the system use? (Example: 25% of the server memory)

- Will users use a LAN or a WAN?

- If WAN, Internet or leased line?

- What is the bandwidth, latency, and packet loss?

- Exception Handling: How should the system respond if an exception occurs? For example, if the number of users exceeds the maximum, a message appears: "System is temporarily unavailable, try again later."

> Note 12: If the customer already has a running system, you can refer to the IS log to get a sense of the transactions volume.

Security

Where applicable, document the following:

Authentication

- How will the system authenticate users? Passwords are most commonly used, though authentication using smart cards, photos, or fingerprints are other possibilities.

- How will passwords be structured? Are there any specific characteristics for the passwords? For example, must they be of a particular length, combination of numbers with letters, a mix of capital with lower case letters (case sensitive)?

- How many failure attempts will be allowed for the user if he/she can't get the password right? Will the system allow the user to retry login using the wrong passwords endlessly or should it block access after a certain number of attempts?

- If the system will block access after a number of invalid trials, what happens next? How will the user recover the password? Will the system send them a new password by SMS or email, for example?

Sensitive Data

- Is there any sensitive data that the system is required to protect (such as high-ranking officials' personal data or credit card numbers)?

- Against what should the data be protected? Only manipulation (add, edit, or delete)? Or should viewing of the data be also prohibited?

- How serious is the threat risk? How important is it for the client's business to protect the data? What will the client lose if the data is exposed (reputation, money, credibility)?

- Exception Handling: What happens if a breach is attempted or if the system fails in any aspect of the security?

Communicate with the technical team regarding the solutions they have (for example HTTPS, SSO, encryption, certificates, etc.) and document them. Make sure the customer accepts the solutions.

System Conventions

If the system is required to use specific conventions such as a UI template or a special CSS, explore that here. Any UI specific standards related to the client organization should be captured. Examples:

- System must use the client's standard UI conventions: look and feel.

- The client's logo must appear on all pages.

- The site should list x number of records per page.

- A link to the Homepage shall be accessible from all pages.

- Next and Previous links shall be provided to move between pages.

- All error messages shall be displayed in red.

- Titles shall have this format "Site Name:Page Name".

Usability

If the customer expresses requirements about the system usability, mention them here. Examples:

- Users shall be able to understand the interface without external guidance.

- The length of system messages must be less than three sentences.

Compliance Requirements
Put here any standards with which the system should comply: for example, money-laundering control or cross-border financial transactions.

Availability
Availability requirements are particularly important for online services: websites, cloud, or hosted services.
- What is the acceptable percentage of availability?
- What is the tolerated down time?
- What is an acceptable meantime between failures?

Training and Documentation Requirements
What training or documentation is required by the customer? For example, user manual, installation guide, online help, etc.

Expected Output: Requirement Statements documented in any of the following ways:
- In a separate Qualities Requirements section that lists general quality requirements not related to particular functions, such as the availability requirements or the auto-complete usability feature, which applies to all screens.

- Or within the function requirements they relate to. For example, a special performance or security feature related to a particular function can be placed within the requirements of that function.

IX. Design the UI

Exercise Objective: At this final stop, you use the information you have from previous exercises to complete the user interface. Depending on the work policy, you may be required to produce the UI draft yourself or to cooperate with a usability engineer, human centered design specialist, or graphic designer who performs this task.

What to Ask/Look for: The best way to go about this exercise is to prepare the prototypes and propose them to the client. Consider the screen flows, screens outline, controls and buttons.

Suggested Analysis Tools and Expected Output: Wireframes, Prototypes

Summary

The following table is a summarized view of the Requirements Detailing phase exercises. Use it as a cheat sheet.

Objective	Analysis Tools	Expected Output
Break down the High-Level Requirements	Six Interrogatives	Questions and answers
Analyze the Functions	Use cases, Six Interrogatives, Method H, Flowcharts, Interaction Diagrams	Use Cases, Flowcharts, Interaction Diagrams, Requirement Statements, Procedures textual description
Analyze the Data	Data Dictionaries, Entity Relationship Diagrams, Class Diagrams, Data Flow Diagrams, State Diagrams	Data Dictionaries, Entity Relationship Diagrams, Data Flow Diagram, State Diagram, Requirement Statements
Detail the Business Rules	Business Rules, Decision Tables, Decision Tools	Business Rules Statements, Decision Tables, Decision Trees
Complete the Users Access Rights	Access Rights Matrix	Access Rights Matrix
Detail the Exceptions Handling	None	Requirement Statements, Messages
Complete the Reports	None	Report Design Specifications
Complete the Qualities Requirements	None	Requirement Statements
Design the UI	Prototypes	Prototypes

Table 6

Phase III: Transition Planning Phase
Post Automation Requirements

If you were to add a new piece of furniture in a hotel lobby, you would think beyond the design and production of the piece. Just like you think about its dimensions, durability, material, and colors, you would plan the best way to install the piece without (or at least with minimal) disturbance to the business operations. You would have to consider the best time to deliver and install it, how to remove and dispose of the retiring piece being replaced, test its function in live situations as well as its fit within the environment. Only after the customer is happy with the new setup would you call the project to a closure and declare its success.

The same logic applies to software. If you introduce new software in an operational organization, you must prepare for the transition phase. You must understand any concerns that the client has and also educate them about this sensitive transition period and help them plan the process to move from the old to the new as smoothly as possible. The requirements phase must include this part to avoid surprises at implementation.

The Transition Planning phase is composed of seven exercises that wrap up the Requirements Development effort and prepare for the transition from old to new work methods. They are:

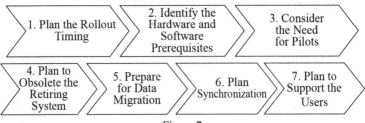

Figure 7

I. Plan the Rollout Timing

Exercise Objective: Timing is crucial in operational organizations. Avoid stressful times so you can introduce the new solution in a relatively relaxed (or at least stable) time, and spare users unnecessary overload. For example, the Annual Budget Closing period or the Yearly Audit month is not a good time to introduce major changes in people's working habits. Perhaps, the summer, when many employees go on vacations, or the second quarter of the year, when the sales team is not so stressed about meeting their yearly targets, are better times. Find out the time constraints and communicate them to the project manager so they can work around them if possible.

What to Ask/Look for:
Coordinate with the project manager and the client, and ask:
- Is there any particular time of the year or month that is generally busier than usual? What about times that are generally slower?

- Are there any upcoming events that may distract users and would not be good times to introduce the new solution? What times are more suitable?

Suggested Analysis Tools: None

Expected Output: Project Plan, Schedule, and Decision Justification

II. Identify the Hardware and Software Prerequisites

Exercise Objective: One of the most unpleasant and avoidable surprises a team may face at the go-live stage of a project is to realize that the environment isn't suitable to run the solution due to issues like hardware or software incompatibility or versions upgrade. The user environment is a point that must be explored early. To be ready to go live, necessary upgrades or conversions must be done in parallel to the solution development effort.

What to Ask/Look for:
- Will the applications be installed on servers or personal computers?

- In either case, do the machines have the needed hardware, capacity, operating systems, licenses, etc.? Get a list of the computers configuration from the client's IT department if possible.

Suggested Analysis Tools: None

Expected Output: List of Environment Dependencies and Prerequisites, and possibly constraints that must be worked around

III. Consider the Need for Pilots

Exercise Objective: It is not generally advisable to do a widespread rollout all at once, especially in cases like:

- Live business operations

- Projects touching core business processes in public service organizations such as government agencies, schools, or banks. The discontinuity of the organization operations could affect large numbers of people or the business' profitability or credibility.

- Large projects that spread over many departments or branches

Careful planning should be applied in general and in these cases in particular.

Geographic Piloting: You may:

1. Roll out the new system only in one site or area
2. Monitor the performance
3. Correct issues that occur
4. Improve the solution or the deployment methodology if needed
5. When all seems fine, deploy at more sites. As you gain more experience and confidence in the solution, the number of deployment sites can be exponentially increased. For example, you may start with one branch in phase one, three branches in phase two, and then grow the number to ten in phase three.

Time Piloting

You can also choose to pilot the new system for a certain period of time to see how it fits into the operational environment and the actual work conditions. You may then withdraw it, correct any issues if needed, and then do a final re-installation.

Feature Piloting

To test the users' appetite to use the system in their daily work, you can introduce some basic features first and then gradually introduce more features in later phases. This helps in discovering accurate information about the users' needs and concerns.

What to Ask/Look for:

- It is better if we introduce new systems in a limited number of places first, not all at once. Is this okay with you? Are there certain sites we can start with? You may choose the geographically closer ones, the more cooperative or more knowledgeable users, the ones that pose lesser (or higher) risks, have less exposure, or less customer interaction.

- Would you like to choose some of your team members to try the system for a week or so as a pilot before going live?

- Which do you prefer: To implement the system with complete features and run all tasks from one system? Or to introduce the basic features first and gradually expand with releases? Recommend what you see as suitable in the situation. As a general preference, gradual deployment is recommended, but you still need to use your best educated guess.

Suggested Analysis Tools: None

Expected Output: Project plan with rollout phases; the project management team is responsible for this plan. Analysts support the team by communicating the client's situation, constraints, and preferences.

IV. Plan to Obsolete the Retiring System

Exercise Objective: Unplanned surprises happen. Don't take the risk and stop a running system before making sure that the new system functions properly. Start by running the new system in parallel with the old system for a defined period of time; monitor the performance, and make sure that the business operations are effectively and efficiently flowing before removing the old system. By doing this, if problems occur, you will be able to correct them without disrupting the business. In the meantime, users will get a taste of the new solution and will build trust in the system capabilities and their ability to use it.

> Note 13: Set a defined deadline to remove the old system. Without a predefined announced deadline, users can be inclined to remain in their comfort zone, working with the familiar system, and never find the need to switch to the new one. Phasing out the old system can take place all at once or gradually by switching off particular components at a time.

What to Ask/Look for: Running both the retiring and the new systems in parallel for some time until we are sure everything works properly and the users feel comfortable with the new solution is a good strategy. Would you like to do that? Do you have any concerns?

Suggested Analysis Tools: None

Expected Output: Project plan with clear phasing out deadlines

V. Prepare for Data Migration

Exercise Objective: If the client has been running other systems, there is a good chance that they will want to transfer data from those systems to the new one for business continuity and knowledge management purposes. This can be particularly useful if the new system provides historical data analysis features that depend on data from previous months or years, such as comparison reports and KPIs.

What to Ask/Look for:
- Are there old data that should be migrated to the new solution?
- What are the sources that the data will be migrated from?
- How far back does this data go?
- Should all records be migrated? What will be needed in the future and what will not?
- How many records should be migrated?
- Should we archive the data that will not be migrated?
- Is there any ground preparation work that needs to be done on the old data before it can be migrated (for example, clean fields or consistency checks)?

Suggested Analysis Tools:
- Data Models
- Data Dictionaries
- Data Mapping Matrix

Expected Output:
- Requirement Statements
- Data Models
- Data Dictionaries
- Data Mapping Matrices

VI. Plan Synchronization

Exercise Objective: If the new system will share data with other systems or run in parallel with a retiring system, think about the synchronization mechanism between the two.

What to Ask/Look for:
- Which data do we need to synchronize?
- How frequently should synchronization take place?
- Should it be automatically initiated real-time or in batches?
- If in batches, is the synchronization automatically initiated at a certain time? If so, when should synchronization take place (which day and time)?
- Should it be initiated upon user request? Where should the option be placed in the system?
- How should we handle existing data that was updated or deleted? Which data overrides the other?
- How should an interruption of the synchronization operation be handled? Should we roll back or stop where the interruption took place?
- If the synchronization fails, does the administrator need notification? How will they be notified?
- Should we log the synchronization event?

Suggested Analysis Tools:
- Data Dictionary
- Data Models

Expected Output:
- Requirement Statements
- Data Models
- Data Dictionary

VII. Plan to Support the Users

Exercise Objective: Transition times are difficult. During deployment and in the early days of operation, users will need different types of support: training, documentation, on-the-job coaching, and emotional support. Your aim here is to highlight those needs in advance to the team, particularly the project manager, and take them into consideration. Ask:

- Should we create reference and educational material for the users?

- Should we produce hardcopy system documentation, online help, video, or audio?

- How accepting or resistant are the users?

- How well-trained are the users in using the technology of the solution? Will the users need training?

- Should we station a team member onsite for some time to support users and answer their questions? Should they occasionally check in?

Suggested Analysis Tools: None

Expected Output:
- Requirement statements that state documentation, training, and change management needs

- Training Plan

Summary

The following table is a summarized view of the Transition Planning Phase exercises. Use it as a cheat sheet.

Objective	Analysis Tools	Expected Output
Plan the Rollout Timing	None	A notification to the PM about stressful and relaxed times
Identify the Hardware and Software Prerequisites	None	Prerequisites presented to both the client and the project manager or owner
Consider the Need for Pilots	None	Plan
Prepare to Obsolete the Retiring System	None	Project plan with clear phasing-out dates
Prepare for Data Migration	Data Models, Data Dictionaries, Data Mapping Matrices	Requirements Statements, Data Models, Data Dictionaries, Data Mapping Matrices
Plan Synchronization	Data Dictionary, Data Model	Requirement Statements, Data Model, Data Dictionary
Plan to Support the Users	None	Requirement Statements, Training Plan

Table 7

SECTION III

COMPLEMENTARY INFORMATION

About the Suggested Analysis Tools

This supplementary section contains a brief explanation about the analysis tools suggested throughout the roadmap. The section is not meant to teach you the tools, but rather to establish a common understanding of the meaning and purpose of each one. If you wish to study the tools in depth, consult the resources listed at the end of the chapter.

First, I introduce you to a fundamental concept that I use to guide the analysis work in an efficient way: the logical building blocks of a software application from a requirements analysis point of view, or requirements analysis aspects.

1. Structuring the Unstructured

From a requirements analysis perspective, software applications handle a number of interrelated logical units.

The following is an illustration of these units. Software applications will have to include some, if not all of them:

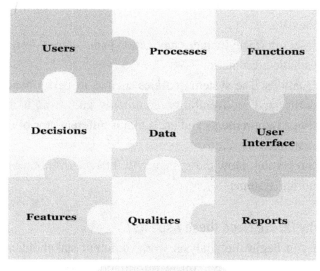

Integration
Figure 8

- Functions: Functions are the core component of a transactional software application. They can be defined as the processing of an input to produce a desired output. They include a part that the user may see and interact with and another hidden part where the system runs its "magic" to achieve the function objective.
- User Scenarios: The sequence of steps a user follows to achieve a goal – often to produce an output from a function. They represent the user experience as they operate on the system.
- Data: The information handled and manipulated in the system functions.
- Business Rules: The rules that govern how the data is manipulated. They are closely intertwined with functions and data.
- Processes: Processes are a series of functions (or user actions) executed by one or more persons, and when completed, produce a result and complete an objective.

- Reports: Consolidated information that offers an insight of the data.
- User Interface: Includes navigation path, screens design, and esthetic presentation.
- Qualities: The system qualities such as its performance, security, and recoverability, commonly known as non-functional requirements and are a major differentiator of quality systems.
- Integration: How the system will interact with other neighboring systems.

2. Why Do We Need these Aspects?

When you begin the analysis work, different stakeholders with different perspectives will throw information at you. Clients don't typically give requirements in an organized way. They tell stories bundled with different types of information: processes they participate in, tasks they execute, business rules they apply, data they consume, volumes of transactions and records they handle, inputs, outputs, processing times, and so forth.

It is your responsibility to structure this information, find patterns, make conclusions, infer untold demands, and prepare to produce suitable solutions. You may feel lost in this information. In fact, this sense of confusion isn't only normal, but also encouraged. Seeing the picture clearly from the start can only mean that you've made early judgments and filled gaps with assumptions. You should approach the problem with a clear, open mind; receive rather than impose. Working with requirements in the beginning of a project is like overlooking a view through a terribly dusty window. The analysis work gradually cleans the window until the picture reveals itself piece by piece. You may have a general expectation of what may be behind the window, but the expectation shouldn't stop you from doing the cleaning – it just helps pose good questions to open channels of discussions and guide the search.

For example, you may expect that the window overlooks a road where there may be trees, buildings, sidewalks, car lanes, lights, parking, bike pathways, and intersections with other roads. There is also the road's attributes: its length, width, and curves. If you have a checklist of the possible items, this will help you efficiently think about all aspects of the requirements.

The checklist shouldn't become a constraint. It should efficiently guide the work, not limit it. The role of the checklist is to ensure that questions are asked at the right time and that the topic is brought up for investigation until an answer is reached and agreed upon by relevant stakeholders before the workers set out to build the road; not to impose a presumed picture. After all, there are many ways to build a road with a different mix of components. A city may, for example, decide to build the drive road from bricks or asphalt, or a pedestrians-only road, or to not include a bike lane.

3. Tools Brief

I will be grouping tools by the analysis aspect for which they are most likely to be used, as follows:

People Aspect:
- Organization Charts
- User Groups List
- Access Control Matrix

Solution Context Aspect:
- Context Diagrams

Processes Aspect:
- Activity Diagrams
- Swimlane Activity Diagrams
- Cross-Functional Flowcharts

Functions Aspect:
- Six Interrogatives
- Use Case Diagrams
- User Stories
- Textual Use Cases (narratives)
- Method H

Decision-Making Logic Aspect:
- Business Rules
- Decision Tables
- Decision Trees

Data Aspect:
- Data Dictionaries
- Entity Relationship Diagrams
- Class Diagrams
- State Diagrams
- Data Flow Diagrams
- Data Mapping Matrix

System Overall View Aspect:
- System Breakdown Charts, also known as Functional Decomposition
- Sitemaps

Root Cause Analysis Aspect:
- Five Whys
- Cause and Effect Diagrams
- Mindmaps

People Aspect

The Users Analysis Aspect focuses on the people who will use the solution, their hierarchy in relation to one another, their characteristics, and needs. The following are the relevant tools.

Tool 1: Organization Charts
Organization charts is a simple hierarchy model that shows the structure and reporting lines of entities, roles, or people. They can be at different abstraction levels: Units or departments, job titles or roles, or people.

Example:

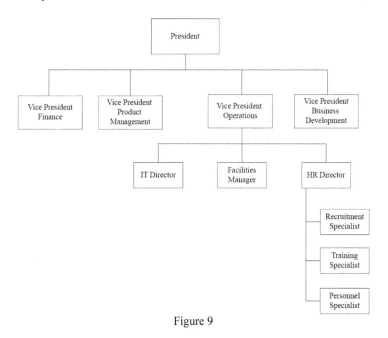

Figure 9

Read more about organization charts in:

- ANTHONY CHEN AND JOY BEATTY, Visual Models for Software Requirements, MICROSOFT PRESS, 2012
- IIBA, BABOK v3.0

Tool 2: User Profile Lists

The list describes the characteristics of the user groups that will operate on the solution, their usage patterns and behaviors, and their objectives.

Example:

User Group	Characteristics and Usage Pattern	General Need from the System
System Administrators	A technical group who will work on the system back end. They have technical experience. Usage Pattern: Regular usage	They will configure and maintain the system. - Maintain Users - Monitor Performance - Print Logs - Manage Templates
Call Center Agents (CCA)	A diverse group of young people with different computer skill levels who work under stress to solve customer complaints.	- Maintain Customers - Report Customer Complaints - Report Back to Supervisors
Supervisors	A senior group who also work under stress to solve CCA problems.	- All functions available to CCA - Monitor CCA performance - Generate Analytical Reports

Table 8

Considerations:

1. Use a consistent name for each group to avoid confusion. Choose one name, identify its aliases, and then stick to the chosen name throughout your documentation and discussions. For example, if you choose to use "Anonymous User" for the unregistered user, keep it consistent.

2. Do not repeat information. If you have the same privileges

for many groups, consider using a matrix that lists the privileges and roles and use checkmarks to map roles to privileges. Alternatively, if one group shares all the privileges of another group plus additional ones, state the privileges of the regular user, and then indicate that the higher user can access the same privileges plus the additional privileges. See the example in table above.

Read more about user profiles in:

SUZANNE ROBERTSON, JAMES ROBERSTSON; Mastering the Requirements Process, 2nd Edition, ADDISON-WESLEY, 2008

Tool 3: Access Control Matrix

A two-dimensional list that shows the user groups on one side and the system modules, functions, or entities on the other. A checkmark or the specific action (such as add, view, update, delete) is typically used to map the two.

Example:

	Sales Executive	Sales Supervisor	Sales Manager	Branch Manager	General Manager
Client Account	View/Add/ Update/ Delete	View/Add /Update/ Delete	View /Add /Update/ Delete	View/Add /Update /Delete	View/Add /Update /Delete
Sales Opportunity	View/Add /Update/ Delete	View/Add /Update/ Delete	View/Add /Update /Delete	View/Add /Update /Delete	View/Add/ Update /Delete
Personal Commission Report	View	View	View	View	View
Department Sales Report	x	x	x	View	View

Table 9

Read more about access control matrices in:

ANTHONY CHEN AND JOY BEATTY, Visual Models for Software Requirements, MICROSOFT PRESS, 2012

Solution Context Aspect

The solution context aspect focuses on the place that the solution occupies in relation to other systems or entities.

Tool 1: Context Diagrams

Context Diagrams are part of Data Flow Diagrams. They represent the highest conceptualization level of a solution and show its relations to other systems or entities outside its boundaries. The Context Diagram is an excellent tool to show integration requirements as they show the data and messages flowing in and out.

Example:

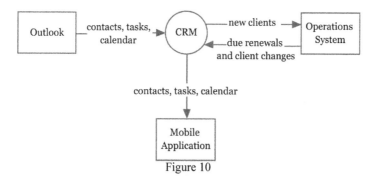

Figure 10

Read more about context diagrams in:

- HOWARD PODESWA, The Business Analyst's Handbook, COURSE TECHNOLOGY, CENGAGE LEARNING, 2009

- IIBA, BABOK 3.0

Processes Aspect

The Processes Aspect focuses on mapping the business process workflows that the solution will fully or partially automate.

Tool 1: Activity Diagrams
They are one of the UML diagrams under the Object-Oriented Analysis and Design Methodology. They show the sequential and parallel steps of a process in a simple representation (rectangular boxes and arrows). They are best used to communicate processes to both developers and users, as they are easy to understand. Example:

Figure 11

Read more about activity diagrams in:

- HOWARD PODESWA, The Business Analyst's Handbook, COURSE TECHNOLOGY, CENGAGE LEARNING, 2009
- IIBA, BABOK 3.0

Tool 2: Swimlane Activity Diagrams
Regular activity diagrams organized using lanes. Each lane is reserved for the actions of one actor.

Considerations:
- You can keep swimlanes simple or borrow shapes from
  flowcharts. I prefer to keep the diagrams simple so they are
  easily understood by all levels of users.
- Maintain a consistent level of abstraction or detailing
  throughout the same diagram as much as possible.

Example:

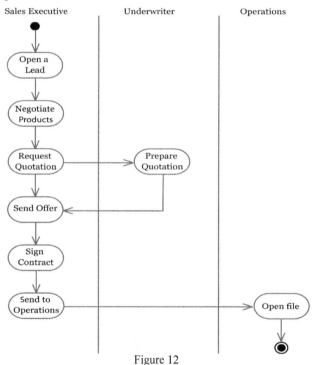

Figure 12

Read more about swimlanes in:
- HOWARD PODESWA, The Business Analyst's Handbook,
  COURSE TECHNOLOGY, CENGAGE LEARNING, 2009
- IIBA, BABOK 3.0

Tool 3: Cross-Functional Flowcharts

Flowchart Diagrams are a more sophisticated type of diagram. With their wealth of notations, they are best used to communicate complex internal system processing logic and procedures to developers – although nothing prevents you from using them to communicate business processes to users who can understand them.

Example:

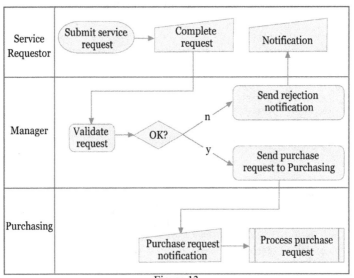

Figure 13

Read more about flowcharts in:

- HOWARD PODESWA, The Business Analyst's Handbook, COURSE TECHNOLOGY, CENGAGE LEARNING, 2009

- IIBA, BABOK 3.0

Functions Aspect

The Functions Aspect focuses on the in-depth analysis of each system function.

Tool 1: Six Interrogatives

The six Interrogatives (also known as the Five Ws and One H): Why, What, Who, Where, When, How. They can be used on all levels of analysis: on the enterprise level, the system level, function, sub-function, task levels, or even on a single requirement statement. Example applied to a transfer fund function in online banking solution:

Question	Description	Example
Why	The root need or the problem that the solution should solve	▪ Reduce work load in banks ▪ Reduce paperwork ▪ Improve customer experience ▪ Speed up transaction
What	The business activity. Think of four "whats": What does the user do now (as-is)? What do they need (the problem that should be solved)? What do they ask for (their request)? What will be done (the to-be)?	▪ As-is: Customer goes to the bank to perform the transfer ▪ The need, the request, and the to-be in this case happen to be the same ▪ Provide an online transfer funds feature
Who	Who will do an action, and who will consume its results or be affected by it?	▪ Registered bank customer ▪ Bank teller ▪ Transfer beneficiary ▪ Audit personnel
Where	▪ The environment in which the work takes place ▪ The scope of implementation across geographical areas and ranches	▪ Online application accessed from anywhere. ▪ Not allowed for cross-border transactions.
When	▪ Timing of delivery ▪ Inclusion in the process	After registering in the online money transfer service
How	The implementation, how will the problem be solved (the design)	Exact functional design details and eventually technical design

Table 10

Read more about Six Interrogatives in http://its.unl.edu/bestpractices/remember-5-ws

Tool 2: Use Case Diagrams

A UML diagram that shows the goals of each actor from the solution; they are good for:

- Scoping a solution
- Showing goals shared between actors
- Showing the interrelationships between different actor's goals

Example:

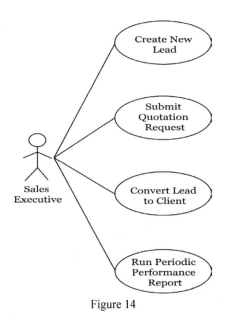

Figure 14

Read more about use case diagrams in:

- HOWARD PODESWA, The Business Analyst's Handbook, COURSE TECHNOLOGY, CENGAGE LEARNING, 2009

- ELIZABETH HULL, KEN JACKSON, JEREMY DICK, Requirements Engineering, 3rd Edition, SPRINGER, 2011

- IIBA, BABOK 3.0

Tool 3: User Stories

User Stories are borrowed from the Agile methodology. You can benefit from the technique, regardless of the project management methodology you are following, to brainstorm with users about the goals they want to achieve from the system. Instead of a tedious objectives list, separating objectives in cards gives you more the freedom to think about the complete picture, see gaps, structure the complete objectives map, and link objectives to one another. Example:

As a Sales Rep, I want to generate my Monthly Commission report	As a Sales Rep, I want to enter my leads to the system with minimal effort
As a Sales Manager, I want to see the Actual to Forecasted Revenues of my department	As a Sales Manager, I want to assign leads to my team members
As a Sales Rep, I want to receive assignments from my manager	As a Sales Manager, I want to create marketing campaigns
As a Sales Rep, I want to upload my business contacts from my mobile phone	As a Sales Manager, I want to add points to my team members

Figure 15

Read more about user stories in:

- MIKE COHN, User Stories Applied for Agile Software Development, 2004
- IIBA, BABOK 3.0

Tool 4: Textual Use Cases

A structured narrative, or a scenario, that describes a user inter-action with the system with the aim to accomplish a goal. Use cases capture the external functional behavior of the system when an actor operates on it. They capture the dialog between the user and the system and therefore should not contain system internal processing (the hidden part of the function).

Considerations:

1. Use cases should be easy to understand. They must be short, focused, and user-friendly so that regular users can read and understand them without difficulty.
2. Use cases should not contain other requirements such as data or non-functional requirements to facilitate future changes. The more you decouple information through categorization and classification, the easier it will be to find a particular component and change it.
3. Use Cases take time to write. They are best used:
    a) For a scenario of a certain sophistication level
    b) To help users visualize an unfamiliar scenario
4. Use Cases can be written as logical representations, show-ing the logical path of behavior without the mention of ex-act control names. For example, when the user submits a request, the system sends the request to the manager for ap-proval. They can also be written to show physical represen-tations citing specific interface controls. For example, when the user presses the Submit button, the system shows the request in the Pending Forms for Approval window.

Example: The following is an example of a physical use case. The scenario is only meant to be indicative of the tool usage and there-fore is not necessarily accurate.

Use Case Name: Add New Contact

Description: The Add New Contact use case describes the possible scenarios that a user may follow in order to register a new contact on their mobile phone.

Preconditions: The contacts repository has been selected

Primary Path:

1. User selects Contacts -> Add New Contact
2. System opens the New Contact form
3. User enters the required data, at least the Contact Name, and presses Save
4. System confirms successful addition

Alternative Paths:

Alternative Path 1:

1. User receives a call from a number that does not exist in their Contacts list
2. User clicks on number
3. System lists available possible options: Add New Contact, Add to Existing Contact, Delete
4. User chooses the Add New Contact option
5. System opens the New Contact form
6. Use Case resumes from step 3 in the Primary Path

Alternative Path 2:

1. User receives a message from a number that does not exist in the Contacts list
2. Use Case resumes from step 2 in Alternative Path 1

Post-Conditions:

1. New contact appears in the Contacts list
2. Contact Name appears when user receives calls or messages from the contact

Read more about Textual Use Cases in:

- ALISTAIR COCKBURN, Writing Effective Use Cases, ADDISON WESLEY, 2000

- ANTHONY CHEN AND JOY BEATTY, Visual Models for Software Requirements, MICROSOFT PRESS, 2012

- HOWARD PODESWA, The Business Analyst's Handbook, COURSE TECHNOLOGY, CENGAGE LEARNING, 2009

- ELIZABETH HULL, KEN JACKSON, JEREMY DICK, Requirements Engineering, 3rd Edition, SPRINGER, 2011

- IIBA, BABOK 3.0

Tool 5: Method H

Neville Turbit of Project Perfect[6] invented the smart technique Method H. Method H is a structured framework that helps analysts partition functions and dissect them for better analysis. The method uses the letter "H" to represent five components of a function: input, functionality, business rules, data, and output.

Considerations: Method H was originally introduced as an elicitation tool, but it proved to be a powerful tool to analyze functions as well.

Example (from Project Perfect):

	Functionality	
	- Check credit rating	
	- Check stock availability	
	- Reserve stock	
	- Backorder stock	
	- Prepare packing slip	
	- Advise accounts of order value	
	- Confirm to customer	
Inputs	**Business Rules**	**Outputs**
- Orders	- Don't process if over credit limit	- Packing Slips
- Customers		- Credit Advice
- Credit Rating	- Check with client before backorder	- Order to Accounts
- Stock Levels		- Confirmation to Customer
	Data	
	- Clients	
	- Order	
	- Backorders	
	- Packing slips	
	- Stock	
	- Credit limits	
	- Order estimated value	

Figure 16

Read more about Method H in:

http://www.projectperfect.com.au/info_method_h.php

---

6 http://www.projectperfect.com.au/info_method_h.php

Decision-Making Logic Aspect

The Decision-Making Logic Aspect focuses on the business rules that govern the operations in the business subject to automation.

Tool 1: Business Rules

Business rules can be constraints, computations, and conditional behavior. They are best communicated as structured text.

Example:

- Constraint: A customer can have only one promotion per payment cycle
- Computation: Order Total = Order Lines Total + Tax – Discount
- Condition:
    - If loan exceeds 1000, it must be approved by CFO
    - If order total is between 1000 and 1999, discount rate is 10%
    - If it exceeds 2000, discount rate is 15%

Read more about Business Rules in:

- HOWARD PODESWA, The Business Analyst's Handbook, COURSE TECHNOLOGY, CENGAGE LEARNING, 2009
- IIBA, BABOK 3.0

Tool 2: Decision Tables

A Decision Table is a technique used to map complex multi-factored decisions. It is a matrix that lists conditions, choices within each condition, and possible outcomes.

Example:

Conditions	Choices							
	1	2	3	4	5	6	7	8
Has bad credit history	Y	N	N	Y	Y	N	N	Y
Has another loan	Y	N	Y	N	Y	N	Y	N
Salary or bank funds => loan installment	Y	N	Y	Y	N	Y	N	N
Outcomes								
Give loan			X			X		
Deny loan	1	X		1	X		X	X
Give conditional loan	2		X	2				

Table 11

Read more about Decision Tables in:

- HOWARD PODESWA, The Business Analyst's Handbook, COURSE TECHNOLOGY, CENGAGE LEARNING, 2009

- ANTHONY CHEN AND JOY BEATTY, Visual Models for Software Requirements, MICROSOFT PRESS, 2012

- The Decision Model: A Business Logic Framework Linking Business and Technology, Barbara Von Halle and Larry Goldberg, 2010

- KENDALL AND KENDALL, Systems Analysis and Design, 5th Edition, 2002

Tool 3: Decision Trees

Decision Trees are another technique used to visually model complex decision-making processes. This technique models the path of choices a user may take to complete a goal in a specific chronological order. It is often used to represent in Interactive Voice Response (IVRs).

Example:

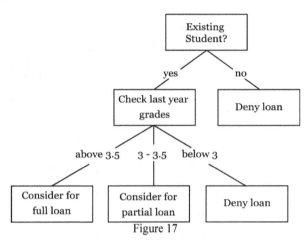

Figure 17

Read more about Decision Trees in:

- HOWARD PODESWA, The Business Analyst's Handbook, COURSE TECHNOLOGY, CENGAGE LEARNING, 2009

- ANTHONY CHEN AND JOY BEATTY, Visual Models for Software Requirements, MICROSOFT PRESS, 2012

- BARBARA VON HALLE & LARRY GOLDBERG, The Decision Model: A Business Logic Framework Linking Business and Technology, 2010

- KENDALL AND KENDALL, Systems Analysis and Design, 5th Edition, 2002

Data Aspect

The Data Analysis Aspect focuses on the data processed in the solution. Data aspects can be static or dynamic. Each aspect can benefit from certain analysis tools, as follows:

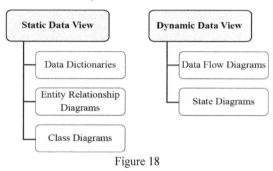

Figure 18

Tool 1: Data Dictionaries

Data Dictionaries are repositories of a system's logical business objects. A business object, or a data entity, is defined as a logical grouping of certain data elements. For example, customer profiles are entities that contain the following elements: ID, name, DOB, and address.

Data Dictionaries are composed of the following four categories:

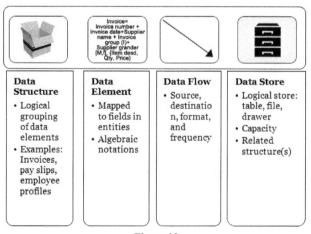

Figure 19

In the Requirements Sketching phase, you produce a high-level data dictionary (a skeleton). This skeleton lists all entities with their elements only without specifying the configuration of each element. In the Requirements Detailing phase, you complete the data dictionary, add the configuration details of each element, and describe data flow and data stores, if needed.

Example: Some people prefer to use a separate column for each property of the data elements, as follows:

Element ID	Name	Desc.	Manda-tory?	Data Type	Length	Format
CST01	Customer Number	A serial number	Yes	Numerical	7	
CST02	Customer Name		Yes	String	30	
CST03	Join Date		Yes	Date	10	xx/xx / xxxx

Table 12

Others combine properties as follows:

Element ID	Name	Description	Properties	Business Rules (if any)
CST01	Customer Number		Numeral (10) Auto-generated Mandatory	
				Viewed by Sales Representatives and Managers Updatable by Managers only

Table 13

Read more about Data Dictionaries in:
- ANTHONY CHEN AND JOY BEATTY, Visual Models for Software Requirements, MICROSOFT PRESS, 2012
- KENDALL AND KENDALL, Systems Analysis and Design, 5th Edition, 2002
- IIBA, BABOK, 3.0

Tool 2: Entity Relationship Diagrams

Entity Relationship Diagrams (ERDs) are used to model the relationship between data entities (objects). Relationships can be association (when an entity is linked to another) or inheritance (when an entity is a child or subset from another parent entity).

Example:

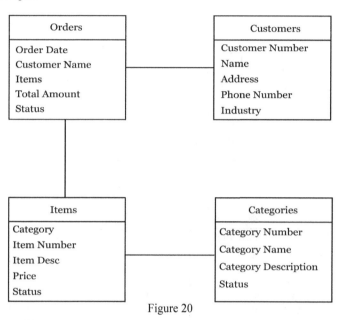

Figure 20

Read more about ERDs in:

- HOWARD PODESWA, The Business Analyst's Handbook, COURSE TECHNOLOGY, CENGAGE LEARNING, 2009

- IIBA, BABOK 3.0

Tool 3: Class Diagrams

A UML Diagram from the Object-Oriented Analysis and Design Methodology. It shows the hierarchy of objects in the system, along with their attributes and the possible operations that use them. Class diagrams show how objects are linked together and relate to each other. They may be used in place of ERDs.

Example:

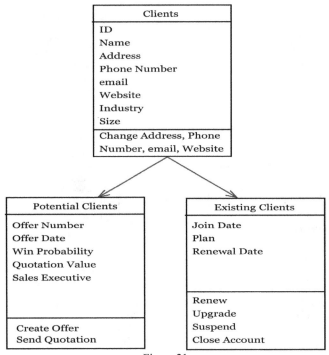

Figure 21

Read more about Class Diagrams in:

- HOWARD PODESWA, The Business Analyst's Handbook, COURSE TECHNOLOGY, CENGAGE LEARNING, 2009

- ELIZABETH HULL, KEN JACKSON, JEREMY DICK, Requirements Engineering, 3rd Edition, SPRINGER, 2011

- IIBA, BABOK 3.0

Tool 4: State Diagrams

Another UML Diagram from the Object-Oriented Analysis and Design Methodology, showing the different states an object can be in and the transitions between those states.

Example:

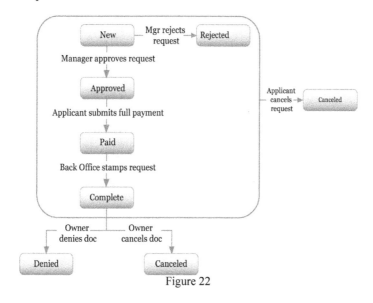

Figure 22

Read more about State Diagrams in:

- ANTHONY CHEN AND JOY BEATTY, Visual Models for Software Requirements, MICROSOFT PRESS, 2012

- HOWARD PODESWA, The Business Analyst's Handbook, COURSE TECHNOLOGY, CENGAGE LEARNING, 2009

- ELIZABETH HULL, KEN JACKSON, JEREMY DICK. Requirements Engineering, 3rd Edition, SPRINGER, 2011

- IIBA, BABOK 3.0

Tool 5: Data Flow Diagrams

A diagram from the Structured Systems Analysis and Design Methodology, these show the flow of data and the changes that take place on the data as it moves through the system functions.

Example:

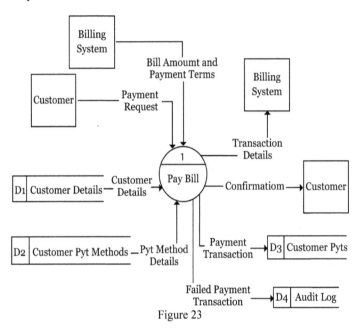

Figure 23

Read more about DFDs in:

- ANTHONY CHEN AND JOY BEATTY, Visual Models for Software Requirements, MICROSOFT PRESS, 2012

- HOWARD PODESWA, The Business Analyst's Handbook, COURSE TECHNOLOGY, CENGAGE LEARNING, 2009

- KENDALL AND KENDALL, Systems Analysis and Design, 5th Edition, 2002

- ELIZABETH HULL, KEN JACKSON, JEREMY DICK, Requirements Engineering, 3rd Edition, SPRINGER, 2011

- IIBA, BABOK 3.0

Tool 6: Data Mapping Matrices

Data Mapping Matrices list the fields that should be migrated or synchronized from one system or version to another. The matrix may list the field description and format, which field they map to in the new system, and the challenges or preparations needed to complete the migration.

Field Name	Description	From	Challenge and Notes
Start Date of the Group	Original start date of the group	Invoices/ Startdate	Only the Group Start Date will be captured, which means the exact start date of each individual within the group will be lost.
Renewal Date		Invoices/ren Month – rendate	Renewal date is called product date in the new system
Payment Amount	Monthly actual payments, divided by month/year	Invoices/pay ment value	Monthly actual payment
	(ex: 1,350 Jan 14)		These are multiple columns for each month
			Note: The due amount is in the Statement column

Table 14

System Overall View Aspect

The System Overall View Aspect focuses on the bird's eye view of the system with its main components without detailing any of them.

Tool 1: System Structure Breakdown Charts

The System Structure Breakdown charts (also called Functional Decomposition Diagrams) are visual models of a system anatomy. They resemble Organization Charts and ERDs in that they show the hierarchy of the system's components and sub-components.

Example of functional decomposition:

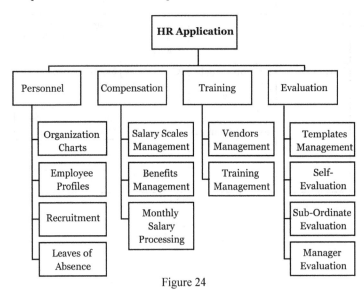

Figure 24

Example of website map:

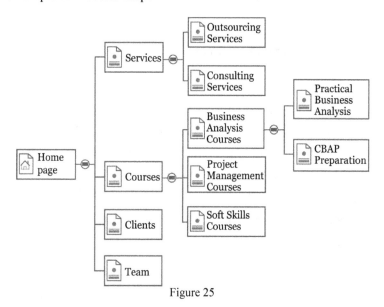

Figure 25

Read more about Functional Decomposition in: IIBA, BABOK 3.0

Root Cause Analysis Aspect

The Root Cause Analysis deals with the aspect of analyzing be-yond the apparent problem to reach the root problem.

Tool 1: Five Whys

Five Whys is simply the process of asking "why" for five times consecutively in order to get to the origin of a problem. The num-ber five is only suggestive. Often the issue is clarified after two or three whys, although the process can also go beyond five times.

Five Whys aims to reveal the underlying problems under the prob-lems apparent on the surface.

Example:

- Why do we need to automate this process? Because the time to delivery is too long.
- Why is the time so long? Because employees spend a lot of time chasing suppliers to deliver their components on time.
- Why do suppliers take so long to deliver their components? There are no contract mandates that enforce them to deliver on time.
- Why isn't there one? Because the legal department didn't mandate that in the company's policy.
- Why didn't the legal department mandate that? When the company started, the only supplier was a sister company, and it wasn't a problem.

You can see that the problem roots go beyond the automation of the process.

Read more about Root Cause Analysis in:

- HOWARD PODESWA, The Business Analyst's Handbook, COURSE TECHNOLOGY, CENGAGE LEARNING, 2009

Tool 2: Cause and Effect Diagrams

Also known as Ishakawa or Fish Bone Diagrams, these show one line that represents a problem and many lines that branch out of that line, with each line indicating a category of the problem.

Considerations: These are best used in complex problem definition cases. Example:

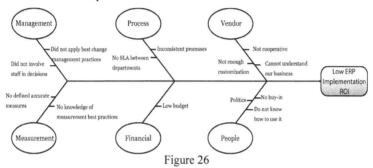

Figure 26

Read more about Cause and Effects Diagrams in:
HOWARD PODESWA, The Business Analyst's Handbook, COURSE TECHNOLOGY, CENGAGE LEARNING, 2009

Tool 3: Mind Maps

Mind mapping is a useful tool that can be applied in different situations. They are useful to analyze information and present them in a graphical representation.

Considerations: You can use Mind Maps to brainstorm issues, organize information, and analyze the possible causes of an issue.

Example: See the Functional Decomposition and website map examples.

Read more about Mind Maps in: SUZANNE ROBERTSON, JAMES ROBERSTSON, Mastering the Requirements Process, 2nd edition, ADDISON-WESLEY, 2008

Case Study

To illustrate the method proposed in the roadmap, I will use the case of a fictional analyst called Maria. Maria was hired by a consultancy company to take care of the business analysis activity on a Customer Relationship Management (CRM) system for a fictional insurance company that goes by the name "FIC".

This is how Maria moved through the exercises outlined in the roadmap to define and produce complete requirements.

Business Analysis Phase

Exercise 1: Know your client

Maria began by asking her hiring consultancy company about the client's business, size, market niche, and culture. Before even meeting with them, she visited the client's website, looked them up online, and read some articles that mentioned them. When she met with the CEO, she was already aware of the published company direction. She began the discussion from a common ground but also made sure she verified the knowledge she had acquired. She asked the CEO to give her an idea about the company vision, coming years' goals, and foreseen challenges.

Exercise 2: What they want and why they really want it

The CEO delegated the project ownership to the Business Development Manager (BDM). Maria sat with him after she met with the CEO and asked the first fundamental questions: "What do you want to accomplish from the project?" and "Why do you need it?"

This was the BDM's answer: "I need to have more visibility and control over what is happening in my department. At any one point in time, it seems difficult to know who is working on which account and how they are progressing."

The answer is good but not enough. Maria didn't close the discussion at that point as she knew this was only the tip of the iceberg; she needed to understand what is behind "visibility and control," the specific needs and pain points, so she made sure they communicated with the solution team and addressed in the solution. She noted the answer he gave her, but still pressed on with more probing questions to get more details (see the questions listed under What to Ask/Look for: this exercise).

The probing resulted in an elaborate and comprehensive list of needs. This list will better guide the project towards a successful, useful solution:

1. Modernize and standardize the administration and execution of the sales process to keep up with the growing competition.
2. Speed up the sales process.
3. Reduce the administrative overhead through partial automation of the process (Maria will soon have to understand what "partial" means).
4. Provide a centralized, consistent data source.
5. Enable managers to track employees' objectives and performance and assess the overall organization strategies based on concrete ROIs to make sound decisions.
6. Reduce human errors.
7. Provide better control over responsibilities and data manipulation.
8. Establish individual-independent processes.
9. Prepare for seamless, end-to-end processes by allowing for integration with other departments systems.

Exercise 3: Understand the present state

Maria wanted to understand the business operations that may be impacted by the new solution. She used the information that she had acquired from the initial research she did on her own in the first exercise about the company's services and products, customers, and markets as a starting point.

Now, she wanted to understand the people in the company. She asked the BDM to show her the company's organization chart. She also verified the organization chart with the HR department to make sure it was accurate and up-to-date. She learned about the number of employees, the nature of their work, and their relationships to each other and to other teams. She asked about the skills of the team members and how much they interacted (or want to interact) with technology.

Maria then met with the head of the IT department to understand the existing map of the technology infrastructure and IT systems. She asked about:

- Servers configuration and distribution
- Network connections
- Operating systems and browsers
- Applications and tools that the users formerly ran on their operations (she also asked this question to the users, just in case individuals unofficially used other tools)
- Files organization and backup system

Maria asked the IT team and the users about what they thought was challenging in the existing solutions. She found out that a past attempt to build a consolidated data repository failed due to data inconsistencies. She now knows that this factor must be put into consideration as they prepare for data migration to the new solution. However, Maria was careful to not get too involved in this issue at this stage. She didn't want to lose focus. She kept it as an open issue and moved on.

Of course, Maria didn't forget to ask what was good about the current system to carry over the strength points to the new solution.

To understand the applied work methods, when she met with the sales team (who are the new solution's users), she asked: "Tell me what your typical day at work looks like. What do you do? What kind of activities do you perform? What else do you do apart from the typical activities? Which activities do you think are the most challenging?"

She understood the steps of the tasks they work on in detail. Inconsistent ways of doing the same activity were identified, documented, and brought to the attention of the manager to decide if there was a need to standardize them and the best way to use in automation.

The output from this exercise was a description of the as-is situation outlined in the following way:

1. A list of team roles and responsibilities (good information that will be used later to define the system user groups in details).
2. Documented processes that describe how work runs (the processes will be used later as categories to organize the requirements elicitation and documentation effort).
3. Current technology model and description, including hardware, operating systems, applications, versions, and network capacities.

The client loved the deliverable Maria presented at the end of this phase. They deemed it a valuable resource that they can use for other purposes as well, such as training of newcomers, presenting the department work to other teams, or as a reference to initiate other projects. Maria also benefited greatly from the previous exercises because she was able to build a rapport with the different stakeholders and understand their work, concerns, and needs – all within a comfortable non-threatening environment.

Automation Requirements Sketching Phase

Exercise 1: Define the Solution Personas

Maria took little time to complete this exercise; she already had information about the users from the Understand the Present State exercise in the Business Analysis phase. She could identify the main user groups of the solution from the players of the processes (for example, the sales representatives and sales managers). She still wanted to confirm the information she had and explore if there were other direct or indirect users of the solution.

As she discussed the issue with the team, a new role that didn't appear in the as-is process emerged. The office manager needed to access certain information, perform some administrative tasks, and generate reports on behalf of the managers.

Because Maria understands technology operations, she proposed a system administrator role to perform system maintenance. Now the list was complete.

Exercise 2: Determine the Users Hierarchy

Maria examined the hierarchy of users that she had from Phase I. She analyzed the depth of the hierarchical levels, the reporting lines between the roles, and the need to give managers the flexibility to skip levels of approvals or view data that belongs to other managers.

Analysis showed that she could re-organize the groups in a way that made sense from a solution perspective. She divided the managers group into immediate managers, higher managers, and top managers, and consolidated the junior and senior sales reps into one Sales Representatives group.

She didn't worry about the users' specific access rights; this would have been too detailed at this high-level stage.

Exercise 3: Find out the Goals of each Persona

From the users' job description and responsibilities, Maria had a good idea about the possible needs they would likely have from the solution. To make sure she covers everything, she met with a sample group and asked them to list what they would like to use the solution for.

Maria used the processes she documented in the Business Analysis phase to guide the discussion around one process at a time.

Although the project did not run on Agile, she still used the user stories concept; each one in the group was given cards to write down their goals. The goals were then discussed in the group, consolidated, and organized. When she was done with all the processes, she explored other goals that were not linked to any particular process (the chores tasks), such as Calendar and Contacts Management features, plus some additional reports.

The project manager was present in that workshop and worked with her and the team on the prioritization of the goals.

Maria made sure the discussion didn't go into the details of any particular goal. The workshop objective was only to identify the goals titles for each user group. If unsolicited details were mentioned and didn't seem to overtake the discussion, she took note of them and returned the discussion towards the main point.

The following is a sample of the result produced from this exercise: The manager will use the solution to:

1. Track team members and overall team progress
2. Generate reports and KPIs
3. Combine team(s) monthly commission reports
4. Review each sales rep monthly commission report

Exercise 4: Explore the Goals Arrangement and Interrelationships

Here, she toyed around with the user stories to arrange them into logical story lines and identify the associations between them. The user stories technique was particularly useful. Having the goals as independent objectives on separate cards, she could analyze them better and quickly spot the associations between them.

This exercise helped her arrange requirements in a meaningful way, identify goals that were overlooked, and find the relationship among the goals.

Exercise 5: Identify Information Needs

From the user goals, she picked some data objects. For example, sales representatives worked with leads (potential customers), opportunities (promising potential customers whom the sales representatives are actively in contact with), and existing customers. They were three subs of the main entity "customer."

She compiled a complete list of objects and set out to explore the elements of which they are composed. She used the forms that the client used as guidance, and then asked the team to review the elements and decide if they need to add or remove elements.

She carefully studied them to see if the elements contained any hidden traps, such as the need to validate a field from another system, but she didn't dive into the detailed properties of each element – that part belonged to the Requirements Detailing phase.

Exercise 6: Find out the Context

Naturally, the discussion that took place during the Business Analysis phase about the existing systems raised the question, "Which other systems will the new system interact with, either directly or indirectly?" Maria asked the IT department, the Sales team, and the Operations department that worked closely with the Sales team. The result was:

- The Sales team expressed a strong need to link their business contacts and calendar from MS Outlook with the new solution.
- They also expressed a need to transfer data between their mobile phones and the solution, so that they can give updates on their progress from anywhere.
- The Operations team planned to automate their operations in the near future. Integration between the two systems was essential.

Exercise 7: Assess the Complexity of the Decision-Making Logic

From the user goals and the information entities exercises, Maria could spot a good number of business rules. Now she needed to take a closer look and assess how complex these business rules are. Most processes applied business rules of average complexity. The complexity was mainly in the Quotation process.

Maria didn't detail the complete exact rules; she just mentioned that they were of high complexity and included a rough estimate of the number of permutations. She categorized the rules in three groups: very complex, complex, and simple. She mentioned roughly how many rules there are in each group, and included a sample of an average case in each group to help the solution team get a clearer picture of the involved complexity.

Exercise 8: Explore Reporting Needs

Sales reps needed a few reports, but most reports requirements came from the managers. Maria didn't worry about the reports design, but only reported their names and purposes, and scanned over their content to ensure they could be produced from the information captured in the system. She checked the information entities to see if they included or allowed for the computation or extraction of the information that the reports were required to show.

Exercise 9: Ask if there is Existing Data

The team used Outlook and Excel to maintain their data and run transactions. There will be a need to migrate this data to the new solution, especially since the reports required by the managers must take into consideration historical data from previous years to be able to consolidate numbers and compare performance.

Maria asked the IT department to help her determine the number of stored records, the location of the files, and the best mechanism to identify duplicates. She also looked in the files and identified the elements that need work. The team members helped her understand how they used each field.

After discussions with the project team and the users, due to the complexity of work required to clean the inconsistent data, a decision was made by the project owner to migrate the records from only the last two years to reduce the volume of migrated data and contain the effort involved.

Exercise 10: Identify the Desired Solution Qualities

With regards to capacity, the number of users who will use the system is limited, so there was no need to worry about the capacity of the concurrent system usage. However, Maria knew that the number of records that will be stored and handled in the system would be large, so she asked the Operations department and the Business Development Manager to give her an estimate of the existing number of clients, and asked the Sales team about the number of leads and opportunities that they stored on their personal computers. She also asked about their future growth plans and their coming years' forecast. The company had already implemented a large database engine, so there was no need to worry about the number of stored records.

From a security standpoint, the Sales team members weren't supposed to see each other's commissions and deals. This concern was going to be handled using passwords, access constraints, and logging.

Exercise 11: Ask about any Specific Technology Mandates

The client didn't have a specific requirement for the technology, except for the database engine, as they had already bought one. Maria documented a requirement to integrate with the existing database.

Requirements Detailing Phase

Exercise 1: Break Down the High-Level Requirements

Maria set out to analyze in detail the body of requirements that she had from the previous phase. She applied the six interrogatives on every high-level requirement to defragment it and raise more questions. This is how she did it:

- Req1: Sales Reps shall be able to create Renewal Opportunities.
- Req2: System should also auto-create Renewal Opportunities.

Why
The need to automate renewals was raised in the user goals exercise from the last phase. Renewals were where most problems occurred for the business. It therefore made no sense to build a solution without addressing this area.

What

Question	Answer
What do you do now (as-is situation)?	Renewing client accounts is a mess. Sales reps often forget renewals due dates, which causes loss of clients. Because there is no clear process to handle renewals, the sales rep used a work-around. They re-open the old opportunity of the client and change the date of renewal to extend the membership for one additional year.
What do you want (what they ask for)?	The team wanted reminders at least two months ahead of a renewal due date.
What do they really need?	A mechanism to ensure renewals are done at the right time to relieve the team from the pressure of keeping track of dates and avoid errors.
What will the solution do?	There were two options: - Send notifications to the sales rep two months before a client's renewal due date and let the user create the renewal opportunity. - Automatically create the renewal opportunities for them and link them to the relevant client record, then notify the sales rep.

Table 15

Who

Remember that it's good to ask this question in both the affirmative and the negative modes: for example, who can or will and who cannot or will not.

Question	Answer
Who will perform the action?	The sales rep, the managers, but not the office admin or the operations team
Who will be impacted by this function?	Clients whose account expiry date is due in two months, and do not have a Deactivated status or do not have the Auto-Renew option checked

Table 16

Where

Question	Answer
Where will the solution be used?	In headquarters and city branches
Where will the function be in the system?	On a special tab on the Sales Reps Dashboard

Table 17

When

Question	Answer
When will this service run?	- Two months before the client's due renewal date - If the renewal date falls on a holiday or a weekend, the two months are calculated on the last working day before the renewal date
When do we need to deliver this function?	Preferably in the second release by mid next year

Table 18

How

This question needed thorough analysis and discussions with the technical team to decide on the exact design of the solution. The next exercises will give some information about the design from a logical user perspective.

The Six Interrogatives opened discussions and provided valuable information that can be used in the subsequent exercises. Maria ran this exercise for each major requirement, and that resulted in a list of questions. Many questions were already answered in the context of other discussions, and not all questions generated useful answers for all requirements, but she still treated the exercise with care to make sure she covered everything.

Exercise 2: Analyze the Functions

Still on the example of the Create Renewal Opportunity function

Maria understood that, in the Create Renewal Opportunity function, there is a level of complexity in both the visible part of the function "the user interaction" and the invisible part "the internal processing." She judged that the best tools to apply are the use cases and Method H.

She ran through a simulation scenario with the team and agreed with them on how the system should respond to the user inputs and choices. She wrote the sequential steps of the use case and the potential constraints, then determined the closing point of the scenario and the expected post conditions.

She then drew the letter H on a board and began the detailed analysis of the internal processing.

The following is a rough view of how the method H categorization looked like:

Input	Steps	Output
- Client record (basic info, status, auto-re-new flag) - Renewal due date - System date - Name of assigned sales rep	**Steps** - Run service to check due renewals - Create an opportunity - Populate defined fields (find fields in the data dictionary section) - Show in renewal opportunities page - Send email notification to sales rep - Log transaction **Business Rules** - Do not run this for Deactivated accounts or accounts with auto-renewal option - Run two months before Renewal Due Date **Data to keep** - New opportunities - Date of generation - Log of failed attempts	**Output** - Opportunity with type of "Renewal" with generation date displayed in the Renewal Opportunities tab - Email notification to sales rep

Figure 27

Exercise 3: Analyze the Data

For each data entity (such as the opportunities, leads, prospects, clients), Maria identified the data elements, their properties, and the validation rules that govern them.

What is mandatory and what isn't? What is unique? What is up-dateable? Which field depends on another? What is generated through an automatic calculation? The format of each field, the validations, and so forth.

Exercise 4: Detail the Business Rules

By the time Maria reached this point, she had already discovered many business rules when she analyzed the functions and the data. She still wanted to ask the question separate from any other. She went through the functions and data entities, and for each process and function, she showed the team the rules that she compiled and asked them to think if there needs to be other constraints or conditions.

The exercise was very helpful because the team (especially the manager) could find important conditions and constraints that he had previously overlooked and that he now discovered because this exercise gave him the chance to carefully reflect on how he wants the department operations to run and under which rules. He was able to come up with new rules that were helpful to the business in general.

Exercise 5: Complete the Users Access Rights

Maria identified three levels of user groups. The Sales Rep group, who should be granted access to their own records only, the Supervisors group, who could do everything the Sales Rep does plus access their subordinates records, and the Managers group, who could do everything the Sales Rep could do plus access everybody's record and generate analysis reports.

Exercise 6: Detail the Exceptions Handling

Maria asked the team to tell her about any unusual cases that they have previously come across in their work, cases that were uncommon in their daily work, or exceptions that require special handling. She also checked the clients' complaint records to see if there are any repetitive or special cases that need special handling in the system.

The search led to some exceptional cases. For example, some clients had compound first names. A few of them had compound names in both their first and last names. A few clients resided in different countries, and their localities data had to be captured in the system.

Maria also explored the possible technical issues that may occur. She brainstormed with the IT department and the solution team about the best mechanism to backup the system and what to do if the connection or the system stopped in the middle of a time-consuming operation such as synchronization, migration, or generating auto-reports.

She sought help from the testing team to find cases of users using the system in a non-standard way, such as entering wrong data formats.

Exercise 7: Complete the Reports

This exercise was one of the easiest. Maria took the list of reports from the Requirements Sketching phase and detailed each one. For each report, she identified the items listed in the questions listed under that exercise in the roadmap (such as who can access the report, the currencies, the filtering criteria, the fields, etc.), and then produced a sample layout.

Exercise 8: Complete the Qualities Requirements

She looked into the list of qualities and produced requirements such as the required capacity, security, accuracy in quotation computation, etc.

Exercise 9: Design the UI

Maria met with the assigned usability engineer and went through the requirements. After the UE created the prototypes, they reviewed them together to make sure no requirements were overlooked, and then took the prototypes to the client. This proved to be a very useful step as the client was able to see how things may look like and also encouraged the users and motivate them to look forward to the new system.

Transition Planning Phase

Exercise 1: Plan the Rollout Timing

The sales team is generally busy toward the end of each quarter and particularly busy at the year end as they race to meet their targets. These were not good times to roll out the solution. Maria has also learned that the office where the team sits was going to be remodeled and repainted in the autumn. That time should be avoided as well. The beginning of the following year, when all the remodeling work was over and the team was still relaxed about their yearly targets, seemed the most suitable time to deploy the solution.

Exercise 2: Identify the Hardware and Software Prerequisites

Some of the users' machines had the necessary compatible systems versions and hardware capacity. Some didn't. They needed upgrading or they would be an obstacle for the implementation. When brought to the manager's attention, he agreed to prepare those machines before the due implementation time.

Exercise 3: Consider the Need for Pilots

Because the users were already using a system (Outlook and Excel), they were attached to their old ways and felt uncomfortable and reluctant to switch to the new system. Maria agreed with the project manager to show them prototypes as early as possible to familiarize them with the system.

With this in mind, the project manager also agreed with the client to roll out the first release with the basic features only to help the user get used to it before they make the final switch. This approach was also useful in the bringing out of more requirements and the identification of required changes.

The first release was deployed only in the headquarters – not the branches.

Exercise 4: Plan to Obsolete the Retiring System

Users were going to use their Outlook system and Excel sheets parallel the new solution for one month after rollout to ensure everything is all right before they fully migrate to the new system.

Exercise 5: Prepare for Data Migration

Maria went through all the data sources with their relevant owners and examined the fields; she produced a data mapping matrix. The matrix contained:

- A list of the fields that should be included in the migration from each entity
- The fields description
- The fields format
- The names of the fields that they map to in the new system
- Challenges or preparations needed to migrate each field

Exercise 6: Plan Synchronization

The client needed to synchronize their clients' records between the new system and the Operations department system for many reasons:

- Avoid prospecting already-existing clients
- Give the sales rep access to the client information
- Automatically generate commission reports based on up-to-date client status and payments
- Allow managers to understand the dynamic overall corpo-

rate sales with its continuous growth or shrinking patterns

Maria talked to both teams to learn how many records are added or updated per day to determine how frequently the synchronization should take place, what data to synchronize, and who has the right to change in which data. Together, they made decisions about the best time to run the synchronization service to avoid overloading the servers, how to log the synchronization operation, and how to handle failures during the runs. She also examined the data and identified the fields that need to be cleansed, made consistent, renamed, or added.

Exercise 7: Plan to Support the Users

The team didn't feel the need to have formal documentation for the system. They only required that Maria give them one short training (about three hours) on the first day of rollout and stay around the first two days to answer their questions. They could then call her during the first week if they had questions or ran into problems.

Closing

The Justification behind two sub-phases in the core phase

The distinction between sketching (high-level) and detailing (detailed-level) requirements is crucial to serve many purposes.

1. Audience - It serves the requirements consumers: Stakeholders interested in the requirements typically come in a duality:

a) Managers on one side and doers on the other

b) Client on one side, and solution delivery team(s) on the other

The four groups intersect as shown in the following matrix:

	Client Side (Business Focus)	**Solution Team Side (Technical Focus)**
Managers (High-Level Focus)	Business Managers	Project Managers Architects and Designers
Executers (Details Focus)	Business Users	Developers Testers

Table 19

While all stakeholders are eventually interested in all requirements, each group is likely to look at it from a specific viewpoint, giving special attention to certain kind of information. Their interest in requirements varies in the type of information they need, the timing of receiving this information, the level of summary or detail, and the form in which the information is presented to them. To cater to the needs of all consumers in a way that makes sense to all of them, does not duplicate work, and allows them to make appropriate decisions at appropriate times, you must approach automation requirements from two perspectives: Solution side versus demand side, and management versus doers.

The following illustration shows the information needs map per stakeholder group:

Technical Audience	High-Level Technical Requirements	Detailed-Level Technical Requirements
Business Audience	High-Level Business Requirements	Detailed-Level Business Requirements
	Management/Decision Makers	Executers

Figure 28

2. Time – It speeds up the process: The timing of the information is often as crucial as the information itself. For example, a project manager needs to view the overall solution components and the main and significant-in-size-and-impact requirements early in the project to give an accurate estimate. A solution architect needs to see the overall components to design an architecture layer and make design decisions in the early phases of the project. Developers and testers, on the other hand, begin work on their tasks later than that. This is why you need to provide high-level information as early as possible in the project and explore the detailed requirements in a later phase.

3. Scope - It assists in scope definition and elaboration: Projects begin with a vision, a business need (or a number of business needs) to fulfill. The need is then translated into a number of user demands or requests. Then each of these demands is later expanded to detailed specifications.

For example, the vision may be to improve operational management. The users then make requests related to the automation of certain processes that achieve that vision, such as the Complaint Management process. Later, designers propose a solution to process a certain procedure online, which data components to capture, how to exchange data with other systems, and so on.

Focusing on high-level requirements before getting trapped in details will allow both you and the team to formulate a complete project scope, which naturally leads to better project planning, and safeguards against scope holes that may cause major requirements changes after the solution development work begins. The sooner the major fundamental requirements are agreed on, the safer it is.

4. Better coverage - It permits better analysis coverage: To better organize, analyze, and complete requirements, analysts must keep this "thinking in duality" mindset for the sake of requirements coverage and analysis. The overall big picture must remain in focus in order to stay on track and not lose sight of the project direction (i.e. the project original vision and objectives). On the other hand, everybody knows that the devil is in the details. The smallest bits and pieces related to the lower level operations must be explored and addressed to ensure no information is missed (e.g. the data fields format and specific business rules).

5. Work distribution - It facilitates team management: Work on the big picture is generally more challenging and requires more experience than work done on the bits and pieces of requirements on the detailed level. Separating the high-level requirements from the detailed requirements allows BA managers to distribute work between a team of analysts, and assign the more challenging work to senior analysts and what requires less experience to the less experienced team members.

Parallel Management Activities

This section briefly lists the requirements management activities that may take place in parallel to the application of the requirements development roadmap.

Activity	Considerations
Requirements Management Activities	
Stakeholder Management	Engaging the right stakeholders at the right time using the right method is key to the success of the project. You must work on this from day one and keep working on it throughout the project. Using the exercises in this phase, it is very likely that you have already come across information that could directly or indirectly point you to stakeholders. Begin building your list of stakeholders and think of who should be on the team and the best way to engage them.
Activities Planning and Estimation	This is the right time to start planning for and estimating the various activities that you will perform during the project. Although you might not be able to provide a complete estimate, you will certainly have a high-level idea.
Requirements Tracking	Exercise 2: Find out What They Want and Why they Really Want It will result in a list of objectives. These rationales justify all the solution requirements. Use them as compass points that all the project's requirements should trace back to in subsequent phases.
Scope Definition and Management	At this phase, you will touch on the scope of the work ahead. In fact, discussions in Exercise 3 will inevitably have taken you towards what can be automated and what cannot. Use this information as your scoping starting point. Keep in mind, though, that the scope is not fully complete until you finish the next phase, Automation Requirements Sketching phase.
Requirements Prioritization	Prioritize the high-level objectives that resulted from Exercise 2 and understand which areas or processes are of higher business value or urgency to the organization.

Activity	Considerations
Requirements Management Activities	
Risks Identification and Management	You are already exposed to the core of the client's business at this phase and are most likely already talking to different people. Observe the situation and try to identify the risks that may lie ahead and list them along with their mitigation strategies. Make sure you involve the project manager or project owner in this activity as well.
Sign off and Baselining	None (although you can request a sign off on the as-is description)
Traceability Management	Listing the objectives that you produced from Exercise 2 is the only activity you need to do at this stage to prepare for future traceability.
Change Management	As you talk to stakeholders, you will be paving the road for the change adoption by understanding their concerns, allowing them time to absorb the change, and build a relationship with them.
Requirements Reuse	The output from Exercise 3 can be maintained for re-use by the business or your team in other projects or initiatives.
Requirements Package Preparation	The output from this phase can be a deliverable on its own. This deliverable will eventually be part of the complete project deliverables package.
Process Management Activities	
Process Improvement	You will inevitably notice areas of potential improvement in business processes and procedures, or in any other area of the business, when you work on Exercise 3. You may work with the client and other team members to identify those areas, recommend, and document improvements.

Table 20

Book ends here. Thanks for reading

A Word from the Author

The roadmap I suggest covers a complete end-to-end journey for software projects that are starting from scratch. You can build on it and tweak it to your specific needs if necessary. You can borrow parts in other project types such as upgrades, customization, and change requests projects. Try to follow the sequential order to guide your work.

In this book, I tried to show that the process of requirements construction can be engineered in a systemized way. It is still a start that can be further tuned and refined. Other ways to order the steps may also be as effective.

You are welcome to write a review for this book, or contribute your ideas and real life experiences in applying the roadmap to dahlia@reqmaster.com

Resources

- INTERNATIONAL INSTITUTE OF BUSINESS ANAL-YSIS (IIBA), Body of Knowledge (BABOK) 3.0, INTER-NATIONAL INSTITUTE OF BUSINESS ANALYSIS, 2015

- HOWARD PODESWA, The Business Analyst's Handbook, COURSE TECHNOLOGY, CENGAGE LEARNING, 2009

- KENNETH E. KENDALL & JULIE E. KENDALL, Systems Analysis and Design, PEARSON EDUCATION, PRENTICE HALL, 2010

- ANTHONY CHEN AND JOY BEATTY, Visual Models for Software Requirements, MICROSOFT PRESS, 2012

- SUZANNE ROBERTSON, JAMES ROBERSTSON, Mastering the Requirements Process, 2nd edition, ADDISON-WESLEY, 2008

- ELIZABETH HULL, KEN JACKSON, JEREMY DICK, Requirements Engineering, 3rd Edition, SPRINGER, 2011

- KENDALL AND KENDALL, Systems Analysis and Design, 5th Edition, 2002

- BARBARA VON HALLE & LARRY GOLDBERG, The Decision Model: A Business Logic Framework Linking Business and Technology, 2010

- ALISTAIR COCKBURN, Writing Effective Use Cases, ADDISON WESLEY, 2000

- MIKE COHN, User Stories Applied for Agile Software Development, 2004

www.ingramcontent.com/pod-product-compliance
Lightning Source LLC
Chambersburg PA
CBHW071001050326
40689CB00014B/3438